TIMELINES
OF
HISTORY
VOLUME 1

THE EARLY EMPIRES

PREHISTORY–500 B.C.

GROLIER

an imprint of

■SCHOLASTIC

www.scholastic.com/librarypublishing

Published by Grolier,
an imprint of Scholastic Library Publishing,
Sherman Turnpike
Danbury, Connecticut 06816

© 2005 The Brown Reference Group plc

Set ISBN 0-7172-6002-X
Volume 1 ISBN 0-7172-6003-8

Library of Congress Cataloging-in-Publication Data

Timelines of history.
        p. cm.
    Includes index.
    Contents: v. 1. The early empires, prehistory—500 B.C. —
v. 2. The classical age, 500 B.C.—500 A.D. — v. 3. Raiders and
conquerors, 500—1000 — v. 4. The feudal era, 1000—1250 —
v. 5. The end of the Middle Ages, 1250—1500 — v. 6. A wider
world, 1500—1600 — v. 7. Royalty and revolt, 1600—1700 —
v. 8. The Age of Reason, 1700—1800 — v. 9. Industry and
empire, 1800—1900 — v. 10. The modern world, 1900—2000.
    ISBN 0-7172-6002-X (set : alk. paper) — ISBN 0-7172-
6003-8 (v. 1 : alk. paper) — ISBN 0-7172-6004-6 (v. 2 : alk.
paper) — ISBN 0-7172-6005-4 (v. 3 : alk. paper) — ISBN 0-
7172-6006-2 (v. 4 : alk. paper) — ISBN 0-7172-6007-0 (v. 5 :
alk. paper) — ISBN 0-7172-6008-9 (v. 6 : alk. paper) — ISBN
0-7172-6009-7 (v. 7 : alk. paper) — ISBN 0-7172-6010-0 (v. 8
: alk.paper) — ISBN 0-7172-6011-9 (v. 9 : alk. paper) —
ISBN 0-7172-6012-7 (v. 10 : alk. paper)
    1. Chronology, Historical

For information address the publisher:
Grolier, Sherman Turnpike,
Danbury, Connecticut 06816

Printed and bound in Thailand

FOR THE BROWN REFERENCE GROUP

Consultant: Professor Jeremy Black, University of Exeter

Project Editor: Tony Allan
Designer: Frankie Wood
Picture Researcher: Sharon Southren
Cartographic Editor: Tim Williams
Design Manager: Lynne Ross
Production: Alastair Gourlay, Maggie Copeland
Senior Managing Editor: Tim Cooke
Editorial Director: Lindsey Lowe
Writers: Windsor Chorlton, Penny Isaacs, Susan Kennedy,
Michael Kerrigan

PICTURE CREDITS
(t = top, b = bottom, c = center, l = left, r = right)

Cover
Corbis: Christie's Images b.

AKG-images: Erich Lessing 30b, Robert O'Dea 41; **The Art
Archive:** Musee du Louvre, Paris/Dagli Orti 13b, Natural Science
Academy, Kiev/Dagli Orti 39; **Corbis:** Archivo Iconografico, S.A.
6, Bowers Museum of Cultural Art 42, Burstein Collection 45,
Richard A. Cooke 38, Gianni Dagli Orti 7b, 18, 25, Frank Lane
Picture Agency/ Tony Hamblin 15, David Lees 40, Danny
Lehman 37r, North Carolina Museum of Art 37l, Gustavo
Tomsich 33b, Roger Wood 33t; **Robert Harding Picture
Library:** P.Koch 20; **Copyright J.M.Kenoyer, Courtesy Dept. of
Archaeology and Museums, Govt. of Pakistan:** 21; **South
American Pictures:** Tony Morrison 30-31; **TopFoto.co.uk:** 13c,
UPPA.co.uk 9b; **Werner Forman Archive:** Otago Museum,
Dunedin 12l.

The Brown Reference Group has made every effort to trace
copyright holders of the pictures used in this book. Anyone
having claims to ownership not identified above is invited to
contact The Brown Reference Group.

CONTENTS

HOW TO USE THIS BOOK

INTRODUCTION

The Early Empires tells the story of humankind from its origins to 500 B.C. The book starts with prehistory, the time before the invention of writing, when no historical records were kept. It shows how humans evolved in Africa more than a hundred thousand years ago, and how their descendants spread first through Asia and Europe and then to Australasia and America. Until about 10,000 years ago all shared a similar lifestyle, hunting game and fish, and gathering fruit, nuts, and berries. From about 8000 B.C. agriculture developed, first in western Asia and then gradually across other parts of the globe.

By providing crop surpluses that freed people from the constant quest for food, the agricultural revolution paved the way for the next great step forward: the birth of civilization. Credit for the creation of the first cities and for writing goes to a people whose very existence was forgotten just 150 years ago: the Sumerians, who inhabited the land between the Euphrates and Tigris rivers in what is now southern Iraq. Other early cultures also flourished in river valleys, along the Nile in Egypt and by the Indus in today's Pakistan.

The eastern Mediterranean region in time spawned other great early cultures—Minoan Crete, Homer's Greece, the Biblical Kingdom of Israel. Meanwhile indigenous developments blossomed in other parts of the world. Early village cultures came together to create first kingdoms then empires in China; in Mexico the Olmecs raised monumental sculptures in elaborate ceremonial centers that were the first in the Americas. *The Early Empires* takes their story to the brink of the classical age, when new concepts of art, philosophy, and social organization would be pioneered in Greece and Rome.

ABBREVIATIONS	
mi	miles
cm	centimeters
m	meters
km	kilometers
sq. km	square kilometers
mya	million years ago
c.	about (from the Latin word circa)

A NOTE ON DATES
This set follows standard Western practice in dating events from the start of the Christian era, presumed to have begun in the year 0. Those that happened before the year 0 are listed as B.C. (before the Christian era), and those that happened after as A.D. (from the Latin Anno Domini, meaning "in the year of the Lord"). Wherever possible, exact dates are given; where there is uncertainty, the date is prefixed by the abbreviation c. (short for Latin circa, meaning "about") to show that it is approximate.

ABOUT THIS SET

This book is one of a set of ten providing timelines for world history from the beginning of recorded history up to 2000 A.D. Each volume arranges events that happened around the world within a particular period and is made up of three different types of facing two-page spreads: timelines, features, and glossary pages ("Facts at a Glance," at the back of the book). The three should be used in combination to find the information that you need. Timelines list events that occurred between the dates shown on the pages and cover periods ranging from several centuries at the start of Volume 1, dealing with early times, to six or seven years in Volumes 9 and 10, addressing the modern era.

In part, the difference reflects the fact that much more is known about recent times than about distant eras. Yet it also reflects a real acceleration in the number of noteworthy events, related to surging population growth. Demographers estimate that it was only in the early 19th century that world population reached one billion; at the start of the 21st century the figure is over six billion and rising, meaning that more people have lived in the past 200 years than in all the other epochs of history combined.

The subjects covered by the feature pages may be a major individual or a civilization. Some cover epoch-making events, while others address more general themes such as the development of types of technology. In each case the feature provides a clear overview of its subject to supplement its timeline entries, indicating its significance on the broader canvas of world history.

Facts at a Glance lists names and terms that may be unfamiliar or that deserve more explanation than can be provided in the timeline entries. Check these pages for quick reference on individuals, peoples, battles, or cultures, and also for explanations of words that are not clear.

The comprehensive index at the back of each book covers the entire set and will enable you to follow all references to a given subject across the ten volumes.

TIMELINE PAGES

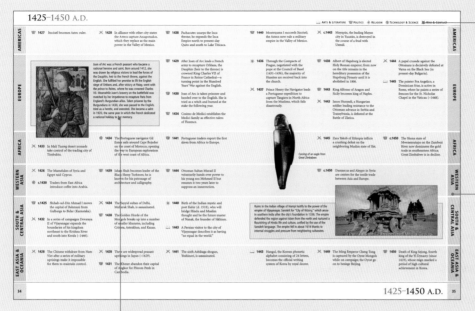

(Sample timeline spread showing bands labeled AMERICAS, EUROPE, AFRICA, WESTERN ASIA, SOUTH & CENTRAL ASIA, EAST ASIA & OCEANIA, with pages numbered 34 and 35)

Symbols

Each entry is prefixed by one of five symbols—for example, crossed swords for war, an open book for arts and literature—indicating a particular category of history. A key to the symbols is printed at the top of the right-hand page.

Bands

Each timeline is divided into five or six bands relating to different continents or other major regions of the world. Within each band events are listed in chronological (time) order.

Boxes

Boxes in each timeline present more detailed information about important individuals, places, events, or works.

FEATURE PAGES

THE OTTOMANS

(Sample feature spread, pages numbered 32 and 33, including a box titled "The Fall of Constantinople")

Maps

Most features are illustrated with detailed maps that put events into their geographical context.

Text

The features flesh out the bare bones of the timelines by providing essential background information on key topics.

Subject-specific timelines

Each feature has a timeline devoted exclusively to its topic to give an at-a-glance overview of the main developments in its history.

PEOPLING THE EARTH

MANY QUESTIONS REMAIN UNANSWERED *about how and when humans first appeared on Earth. But the evidence of ancient skeletons, whose age can be estimated by techniques such as radiometric dating, suggests the first modern humans—known to science as the species* Homo sapiens, *Latin for "wise man"—were living in Africa at least 160,000 years ago. At the time there were other human groups, all of which subsequently died out. The last to go were the Neanderthals, a stockily built people with brains as big as those of modern humans, who survived until about 28,000 years ago.*

▲ Hand axes, flaked from larger blocks of stone, were early humans' most common tools up to about 250,000 years ago, after which more specialized implements came into use.

Early humans fed themselves by hunting game and fish and by gathering fruits, nuts, berries, and (if they lived near the coast) shellfish. They were skillful toolmakers, using the materials at hand—mostly stone, wood, and animal bones—to make axes, scrapers for cleaning animal skins, fishhooks, and a variety of weapons, including spears and bows and arrows. They lived in small bands, typically of 25 to 30 people, that occasionally linked up with neighboring groups in tribes or clans a few hundred strong.

Coping with the cold was a major problem, since the Earth was in the grip of the last Ice Age. Caves provided natural shelters, particularly when warmed by fires. Otherwise the bands had to fashion huts out of whatever materials they could find; in eastern Europe they sometimes used the bones of mammoths (giant elephants that have since gone extinct), covering a bone frame with the animals' hairy hides. They also used animal skins to make clothes.

Moving out from Africa, modern humans reached the Near East between 100,000 and 70,000 years ago, and then spread to the east and west, replacing the existing Neanderthal populations. They had found their way to Australia by 45,000 B.C.; the last stage of that particular migration must have involved a sea journey of at least 55 miles (90 km).

America was almost certainly the last continent to be peopled. Scholars believe the first settlers came

⊛ **c.6.8 m.y.a.** Date of earliest known hominid (human ancestor) remains, found in Chad, Africa, and named *Sahelanthropus tchadensis*.

⊛ **c.6.0 m.y.a.** Estimated date of *Orrorin tugenensis*, discovered in Kenya. The find was nicknamed "Millennium Man" because it was made in the year 2000.

⊛ **c.3.6 m.y.a.** Fossil footprints found at Laetoli, Tanzania, indicate that hominids were walking on two feet by this date.

⊛ **c.3.5 m.y.a.** "Lucy," a female hominid of the species *Australopithecus afarensis*, lived in what is now Ethiopia. Her remains were the oldest yet known when they were discovered in 1974.

⊛ **c.2.4 m.y.a.** Oldest known stone tools, found at Hadar in Ethiopia.

⊛ **c.2.4 m.y.a.** First appearance of *Homo rudolfensis* and *Homo habilis*, currently thought to be the first direct human ancestors.

⊛ **c.1.8 m.y.a.** First appearance of *Homo erectus*, with a brain size about two-thirds that of modern humans.

⊛ **c.1 m.y.a.** *Homo erectus* reaches Europe and Asia.

⊛ **c.400,000 B.C.** Earliest surviving wooden tool, a spear found at Schoningen (Germany).

⊛ **c.160,000** Earliest remains of *Homo sapiens*—the modern human race—found in the Afar region of Ethiopia.

⊛ **c.120,000** Neanderthals living in Europe.

⊛ **c.100,000** *Homo sapiens* moves out of Africa.

Cave Art

From about 32,000 years B.C. prehistoric cave dwellers in France and Spain started drawing images of big-game animals on the walls of the caverns in which they lived. Similar rock art has also been found in North Africa (from a later date) and in Australia. The artists used charcoal to draw black lines, coloring in the outlines with natural pigments ground to a powder and mixed with water. Some scholars have suggested that the drawings may have had magical significance, helping hunters kill the animals represented, although they may also have been sketched simply for pleasure. Only Homo sapiens—the modern human line—is known to have ever produced art. One of the most famous cave-painting sites is at Lascaux, in the Dordogne region of southern France. Dating back about 16,000 to 17,000 years, paintings like those from the Hall of the Bulls (right) show the animals that inhabited the region at the time, including some, like the aurochs (wild ox), that are now extinct.

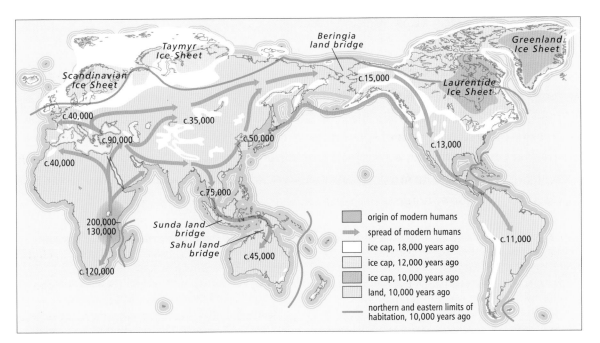

Map labels:
- Taymyr Ice Sheet
- Beringia land bridge
- Greenland Ice Sheet
- Scandinavian Ice Sheet
- Laurentide Ice Sheet
- c.15,000
- c.40,000
- c.35,000
- c.90,000
- c.50,000
- c.40,000
- c.13,000
- c.75,000
- 200,000–130,000
- Sunda land bridge
- Sahul land bridge
- c.45,000
- c.120,000
- c.11,000

Legend:
- origin of modern humans
- spread of modern humans
- ice cap, 18,000 years ago
- ice cap, 12,000 years ago
- ice cap, 10,000 years ago
- land, 10,000 years ago
- northern and eastern limits of habitation, 10,000 years ago

Australopithecus afarensis

Homo habilis

Neanderthal

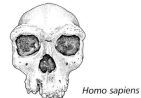

Homo sapiens

from Asia, but disagree as to the date. Most think they arrived about 15,000 years ago over a land bridge linking Siberia and Alaska at the time; but a few claim that they came as much as 40,000 years ago. Here as elsewhere in prehistory the evidence is incomplete; opinions may change as new finds fill out the picture.

▲ Current evidence suggests that modern humans originated in East Africa at least 160,000 years ago and then spread out from Africa to people most of the world.

▶ The size of the cranium (braincase) increased steadily in early hominids up to Neanderthals and Homo sapiens (modern humans), who had similarly sized brains.

⊕ **c. 90,000** Modern humans living at Qafzeh (Israel).

⊕ **c. 75,000** Modern humans living in Southeast Asia.

⊕ **c. 45,000** Modern humans reach Australia.

📖 **c.45,000** Date of earliest known musical instrument—a flute found in North Africa.

⊕ **c. 40,000** Modern humans move into Europe, living alongside the existing Neanderthal populations.

⊕ **c. 28,000** Last surviving Neanderthal population, living in southern Spain, becomes extinct.

⊕ **c. 15,000** Likely date for first settlement of America. Some scholars, however, think people could have arrived as early as 40,000 B.C.

THE AGRICULTURAL REVOLUTION

STARTING ABOUT 13,000 YEARS AGO, *people made the major advance of cultivating plants and domesticating (taming) animals. This great shift occurred independently in West and East Asia, the Americas, and Africa. Although revolutionary in its effects, the change from nomadic foraging to settled agriculture was a gradual one that took several thousand years. Recent research suggests that farming did not necessarily go hand in hand with the development of towns, as formerly thought.*

People first began to raise plants for food as the climate became warmer and wetter at the end of the last Ice Age. In the Fertile Crescent, a swath of land across West Asia, early farmers grew wheat and barley from wild grass seeds. In China the first agriculturalists cultivated wild millet in the north and wild rice in the south. Early inhabitants of Ecuador may have grown squash as long as 10,000 years ago.

The cultivation of plants was accompanied by the domestication of animals—sheep, goats, and cattle in Asia, the pig in both Europe and China. Although there were no mammals suitable for domestication in North and Central America, natives of Peru in South America domesticated the guinea pig about 8,000 years ago and the llama some 2,500 years later.

People did not give up hunting and gathering as soon as they had learned how to domesticate plants and animals. Hunter-gatherers in Syria and China cultivated crops thousands of years before their successors became full-time farmers. There was a

▲ Rock paintings from the Tassili plateau in the heart of the Sahara show that the land was fertile enough to support the raising of cattle around 6,000 years ago, when the paintings were created.

transition to agriculture
- ▓ before 8000 B.C.
- ▓ before 6000 B.C.
- ▒ before 3000 B.C.
- ☐ before 500 B.C.

- ▒ hunters and gatherers
- ☐ uninhabited

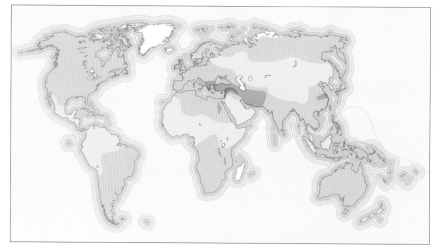

◄ From West Asia's Fertile Crescent region (*purple area*) agriculture spread to the east and west through the world's temperate and tropical zones. In the north and south the hunter-gathering lifestyle survived longer.

► One of the best-preserved Neolithic sites is Skara Brae in the Orkney Islands north of Scotland. Its inhabitants lived on shellfish and the flesh of tame sheep and cattle.

✲ **c.11,000 B.C.** Rye cultivated east of Aleppo, Syria.

✲ **c.8500** Sheep domesticated in Iraq.

✲ **c.8000** Wheat cultivated in Syria and Turkey; barley cultivated in Jordan, Iran, and Israel; squash cultivated in Ecuador.

✲ **c.8000** Pigs domesticated in China.

✲ **c.7500** Goats domesticated in Iran.

✲ **c.7000** Pigs domesticated in Turkey.

✲ **c.6000** Cattle, probably bred from the wild aurochs, domesticated in Greece and Turkey; guinea pigs domesticated in Peru.

✲ **c.6000** Wild rice cultivated along the Chang (Yangtze) River, China.

✲ **c.5700** The first irrigation works are built in Mesopotamia.

✲ **c.5600** Beans cultivated in Peru.

✲ **c.4500** Horses domesticated in Ukraine.

✲ **c.3500** Llamas domesticated in Peru.

✲ **c.3000** Asses domesticated in Egypt; bottle gourds cultivated in Missouri.

✲ **c.2000** Sorghum cultivated in Niger; cereals first cultivated in North America.

simple reason for this slow transition to settled agriculture: While the human population remained small and wild food was abundant, it was easier to make a living by hunting and gathering than by planting, tending, and harvesting crops.

It is harder to explain why sizable towns grew up in this changeover period. Scholars used to think that the first towns were established by farming communities, but recent excavations at 9,000-year-old sites in Turkey show that the inhabitants were at best part-time farmers and may have supported themselves mainly by hunting and gathering.

Towns did grow more numerous and populous when people made the shift to full-time farming—a development probably speeded up by rising populations and overhunting. Faced with such conditions, farmers had one great advantage over foragers: While hunter-gatherers could eat only what nature provided, farmers could increase their output by extending the area of land under cultivation.

Farming seems to have become the main livelihood in parts of West Asia about 10,000 years ago, in China 1,000 years later, and in the Americas and Africa by about 7,000 years ago. By the 4th millennium B.C. some farming communities were producing a food surplus that they could trade or barter for other goods, such as tools or pottery. Once they had reached that stage, people were poised to take the next leap forward—the urban revolution and the establishment of what we call civilization.

The Domestication of the Horse

Of all the animals domesticated by people, none has had a greater effect on history than the horse. When horses were first domesticated in the Ukraine about 6,500 years ago, they were kept mainly for their meat, milk, and hides. The early Babylonians used them to pull wagons, but considered it undignified to ride them—probably because the horses of the period were still small and wild. Although the Egyptians harnessed horses to two-man war chariots, it was not until about 1000 B.C. that individual mounted soldiers appeared. From that time on the horse brought a new and rapid tempo to the way people lived. Horses speeded up overland trade and communication and, as cavalry mounts, dramatically changed warfare, becoming the swiftest form of battlefield transportation until the invention of the tank almost 3,000 years later.

AMERICAS

✷ **c.3000** Potatoes are cultivated in the Andes mountains of Peru.

✷ **c.3000** The earliest known pottery in the Americas is produced in Ecuador and Colombia.

✷ **c.3000** An early form of corn is cultivated in the Valley of Tehuacán, Mexico.

EUROPE

✷ **c.3000** The ox-drawn plow, invented in the Near East, changes the landscape as farmers clear forests to make bigger fields.

✷ **c.3000** Wealth from olive and vine culture encourages the growth of the first towns in the Aegean Sea region.

📖 **c.3000** A marble industry producing fine sculptures flourishes in the Cyclades, a group of Greek islands in the Aegean Sea.

✷ **c.3000** Communities in Scandinavia build passage tombs and dolmens—stone monuments made with blocks weighing up to 40 tons.

✷ **c.2800** The Beaker People, a culture that buries their dead with characteristic earthenware beaker vessels, spread out from Spain to northern Europe.

AFRICA

✷ **c.3000** Yam and palm-oil cultivation develops in West Africa.

👑 **c.2950** Egypt's 1st Dynasty comes to power under the Pharaoh Menes, with its capital at Memphis in Lower Egypt.

Tomb stele of King Wadj from Abydos, Egypt, c.2850 B.C.

✷ **c.2900** Egyptian astronomer-priests devise the first 365-day calendar.

📖 **c.2800** Egyptian scribes begin to write on papyrus made from the crushed stems of a fibrous plant growing along the banks of the Nile River.

WESTERN ASIA

👑 **c.3000** Independent Sumerian city-states flourish in southern Mesopotamia (Iraq).

👑 **c.3000** Non-Sumerian Semitic tribes move into the northern parts of Mesopotamia, settling the plains of Shinar and Akkad.

👑 **c.2900** The Early Dynastic Period gets under way in Sumer as different city-states battle for supremacy, appointing *lugals* (military leaders) to steer their destiny.

📖 **c.2900** The most likely date for the Great Flood, commemorated in Sumerian myth. Archaeological evidence in fact suggests that there may have been more than one such deluge.

👑 **c.2900** The Phoenicians, a seafaring people of the Mediterranean's eastern shore, settle on the Lebanese coast, establishing settlements at Tyre and Sidon.

☀ **c.2900** The first ziggurats—stepped temple-towers—are built in Sumer.

👑 **c.2750** Troy is founded on the eastern coast of the Aegean Sea in what is now Turkey. At this time it is a small walled settlement ruled by a local chieftain.

👑 **c.2750** Gilgamesh rules the city-state of Uruk. He will later enter legend as the hero of the *Epic of Gilgamesh*, the world's first literary classic.

EAST ASIA & OCEANIA

✷ **c.3000** At Banpo in northern China, communities build large meeting houses over 60 feet (18 m) long.

✷ **c.3000** Walga Rock in Western Australia is used as a shelter by Aboriginal hunter-gatherers and remains in use for the next 5,000 years.

☀ **c.2900** According to tradition, the first, mythical emperors of China—divine beings who were half-human and half-animal—ruled from about this time.

AMERICAS

⊕ **c.3000** Natives of western Nevada inhabit rock shelters furnished with skin blankets, baskets, and featherwork.

⊕ **c.2600** Natives of fishing villages in the Chinchorro region on the Chile–Peru border develop a simplified method of mummifying their dead.

EUROPE

Waisted drinking cups with flared lips and incised decorations were the distinctive feature of the Beaker People, who spread from Spain across much of central and western Europe in the course of the 3rd millennium B.C. They were farmers and herders who brought with them knowledge of metalworking, being skilled in the production of copper and bronze artifacts. Their weapon of choice was the bow and arrow, but they also used copper-bladed daggers and spears.

⊕ **c.2800** Neolithic (New Stone Age) settlers at Skara Brae in the Orkney Islands north of Scotland build stone houses sunk beneath ground level and covered with turf.

⊕ **c.2800** Grand Pressigny in western France becomes the export center for a high-quality flint suitable for making knives and daggers.

☀ **c.2800** In England Stonehenge first becomes a ceremonial center. At this date it has none of the giant standing stones for which it will later become famous: only circular earthworks and, perhaps, wooden posts, now long since rotted away.

📖 **c.2700** Early Minoan civilization develops on Crete, reaching its zenith after 2000 with the building of sumptuous palaces.

AFRICA

☀ **c.2650** The world's first massive stone monument, the Step Pyramid, is built for the Pharaoh Djoser.

👑 **c.2575** Egypt's Old Kingdom Period gets under way with the foundation of the nation's 4th Dynasty.

Egyptian scribe writing on papyrus. Old Kingdom Period.

☀ **c.2550** The Great Pyramid at Giza is built as a 480-foot-high (146-m) tomb for the Egyptian Pharaoh Khufu.

WESTERN ASIA

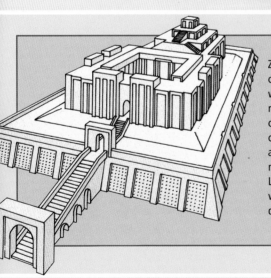

Ziggurats developed out of the Sumerian custom of building temples on platforms; when the mud-brick walls collapsed, the ruins provided a base for a new structure, creating a staggered effect. Over the centuries architects across Mesopotamia adopted this stepped plan, creating temple-mountains that reached toward the heavens. Later examples like this one from Qatara were part of elaborate temple complexes that dominated the cities in which they stood.

📖 **c.2600** Magnificent golden artworks, along with dozens of human sacrifices, are buried in the Royal Tombs of Ur, to be rediscovered by the British archaeologist Leonard Woolley in the 1920s.

EAST ASIA & OCEANIA

⊕ **c.2700** The production of silk from silkworms starts in China.

👑 **2698** Traditional date for the accession of Huang Di, the Yellow Emperor, a mythical early ruler of China.

⊕ **2637** According to later tradition, Year 1 of the Chinese calendar falls in this year.

3000–2500 B.C.

THE SUMERIANS

WHILE MOST OF THE WORLD *lived in caves or huts, the Sumerians created the first urban civilization in southern Mesopotamia—the land between the Tigris and Euphrates rivers in today's Iraq. Their origins are uncertain, but they may have migrated from the Caspian Sea area, reaching Mesopotamia by about 5500 B.C. Over the next 3,000 years they built the first cities, established hereditary kingship, and devised a writing system that made them the first people in history to record history itself.*

▲ Wealthy Sumerians placed small pottery figures of themselves, with their hands clasped in prayer, in shrines dedicated to the gods.

▶ Sumer's heartland lay close to the ancient coastline of what is now southern Iraq. In time Sumerian influence spread northward through all of Mesopotamia.

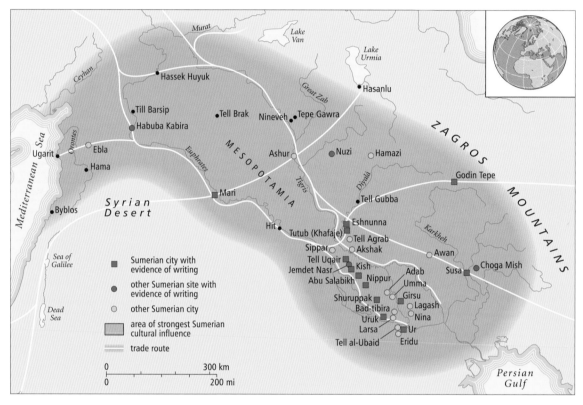

Timeline

⚙ **c.5500 B.C.** The first archaeological evidence of Sumerians in Mesopotamia.

⚙ **c.5400** Advanced farming methods, including irrigation projects, first appear in Mesopotamia.

⚙ **c.3500** The first Sumerian towns appear. Primitive writing is developed.

⚙ **c.3400** Uruk becomes the first large Sumerian city, with an area of at least 500 acres (200 ha) and a population of around 50,000.

⚙ **c.3300** The Sumerians invent the potter's wheel and the plow.

⚙ **c.3000** Early cuneiform writing begins to replace pictographs.

⚙ **c.2900** Parts of Mesopotamia are devastated by a severe flood, an event that may have influenced stories of the worldwide flood described in the Old Testament.

📖 **c.2750** Gilgamesh becomes ruler of Uruk. He will later be immortalized as a semidivine king in the world's first literary epic, the *Epic of Gilgamesh*.

Sumerian Writing

Sumerian writing originated in primitive accounting; merchants and tax collectors inscribed numbers and pictures (pictographs) in wet clay to represent quantities and objects. As time passed, a more stylized system developed in which reeds were used to make wedge-shaped impressions known as cuneiform (from the Latin *cuneus*, "wedge"). Early cuneiform had no grammatical elements; it was only after 2500 B.C. that signs were used to show the order in which words should be read. Finally, symbols that stood for sounds were invented, which meant that scribes could express abstract ideas like "love" or "justice."

The key to the Sumerians' achievements was irrigation. Because Mesopotamia's rivers are unreliable, its people built reservoirs and canals on a grand scale, turning large areas of barren soil into fertile farmland. Crop production was also boosted by technological innovations: The plow, the wheeled cart, and the sailboat are all Sumerian inventions.

Plentiful food supplies led to population increase, the growth of cities, and the opportunity for some people to quit farming for urban occupations. Some Sumerians became merchants and traders, exchanging the region's surplus harvests for the metals, timber, and other resources that Sumer lacked. Others were skilled craftsmen. Many must have been officials working for Sumer's political and religious leaders.

At first, Sumerian cities may have been governed by a council of elders. During times of conflict the council appointed a military commander called a *lugal*—literally, "great man." The position was supposed to be temporary; but as competition for land and water intensified, the *lugals* assumed power permanently and made their position hereditary. Eventually the title came to mean "king."

The Sumerian kings ruled about a dozen independent city-states, each consisting of one or more urban centers surrounded by villages and farmland. At the heart of each city stood the temple of its patron god or goddess. Over time these temples evolved into massive stepped structures, called ziggurats, that rose up to 165 feet (50 m) high.

The Sumerians were also capable mathematicians. As well as counting in tens, they used 60 as an arithmetical unit; from them come our 360-degree circle, 60-minute hour, and 60-second minute. But their greatest contribution was their writing system, used to record everything from business transactions to treaties and laws. Setting words down in writing was a key step because it gave them a status independent of the people who promulgated them.

Despite their accomplishments, the warring city-states were vulnerable to invasion. From about 2350 B.C. on, they were overrun by Semitic tribes from the north. By about 1950 B.C. their political power had been destroyed, but their writing, laws, religion, and much else lived on in the civilizations of such later Mesopotamian powers as Babylon and Assyria.

▼ The Standard of Ur, a mosaic designed to be carried in royal processions, illustrates scenes from a military campaign waged by the powerful city-state of Ur in about 2500 B.C. In this detail cattle, goats, and other tribute provided by the defeated enemy are paraded before a council made up of the city's ruling elders.

👑 **c.2600** Rulers of the southern city-state of Ur are buried in tombs together with their attendants.

✴ **c.2500** Sumerian writing spreads abroad as trade routes are opened.

👑 **c.2350** The Sumerian city-states are overrun by Sargon of Akkad, a ruler of Semitic stock whose power base lies farther north within Mesopotamia. Sargon subsequently establishes the first empire known to history.

✴ **c.2100** From Ur, King Ur-Nammu reasserts Sumerian power, founds schools for scribes, establishes the first legal code, introduces calendar reforms, and promotes international trade.

✕ **c.1950** Ur is sacked by the Elamites from western Iran, bringing the era of Sumerian political power to an end.

2500–2000 B.C.

AMERICAS

⊛ **c.2500** Pottery is made in the lower Savannah River valley of Georgia and South Carolina.

⊛ **c.2500** Natives of valleys along Peru's northern coast build complexes that cover more than 30 acres (12 hectares) and include mounds, plazas, and terraces.

⊛ **c.2400** Hunter-gatherers along North America's east coast catch fish by building weirs of stakes that trap the fish as the tide falls.

EUROPE

⊛ **c.2500** Farmers around the Mediterranean develop the technique of winemaking by the fermentation of grapes.

☀ **c.2300** Construction begins on Europe's largest stone circle at Avebury in southern Britain.

⊛ **c.2300** Bronze, an alloy of copper and tin first made in western Asia around 3500 B.C., is introduced to Europe.

⚔ **c.2200** As competition for land increases, communities in southern Britain build defensive enclosures with timber posts up to 5 feet (1.5 m) in diameter.

AFRICA

The fourth pharaoh of Egypt's 4th Dynasty, Khephren, is remembered today as the builder of the second-largest of the three Pyramids of Giza and also of the Sphinx, which guards it. Here he is shown wearing the headdress and false beard that were symbols of pharaonic authority, seated on a throne topped by a protective image of the falcon-god Horus.

📖 **c.2500** Work is completed on the Sphinx, a 220-foot-long (67-m) monument to the Pharaoh Khephren sculpted from a limestone outcrop.

⊛ **c.2500** The Beaker Culture, so called because of its distinctive ritual drinking vessels, reaches northwest Africa.

WESTERN ASIA

⚔ **c.2500** After defeating the neighboring Sumerian city-state of Umma, King Eannatum of Lagash erects the Stele of the Vultures, a victory monument that sets out the first known peace treaty.

⚔ **c.2350** Sargon the Great of Akkad conquers the Sumerian city-states and creates the world's first recorded empire.

📖 **c.2350** At Alaca Höyük in Turkey rulers are buried with gold jewelry and vessels, along with bronze standards representing stags and bulls, indicating the existence of a prosperous civilization on the Anatolian plateau.

Stag from Alaca Höyük, c.2350 B.C.

SOUTH & CENTRAL ASIA

⊛ **c.2500** In India's Indus Valley cities like Harappa attract a population of up to 40,000 people living in houses with bathrooms and toilets connected to a common drainage system.

⊛ **c.2500** The two-humped Bactrian camel is domesticated in Central Asia.

EAST ASIA & OCEANIA

⊛ **c.2500** Breadfruit trees are cultivated on plots in Southeast Asia and the Philippines.

⊛ **c.2500** Bronzeworking begins to develop from this time on in China.

⊛ **c.2500** Potters in western China learn how to produce superior ceramic vessels by firing fine-grained clay at high temperatures.

AMERICAS

⊕ **c.2400** Cotton textiles of complex design are made at coastal sites in northern Peru.

⊕ **c.2300** Peruvians living at the highland site of La Galgada build plastered stone buildings that include burial chambers for the settlement's elite (ruling class).

EUROPE

Monumental stones at Avebury, England.

⊕ **c.2100** A new stage of construction gets under way at Stonehenge; within the existing earthen bank a massive stone circle, made of blocks weighing up to 50 tons, transforms the site into southern England's major ceremonial center.

AFRICA

⊕ **c.2500** The cat is first domesticated in Egypt.

👑 **c.2250** Pepi II, one of Egypt's longest-lived pharaohs, comes to the throne.

👑 **c.2170** Pepi II dies, and Egypt enters a time of troubles marked by a number of short reigns.

👑 **c.2125** Egypt's Old Kingdom falls apart, and the First Intermediate Period begins, with rival dynasties claiming power in Upper and Lower Egypt.

👑 **c.2040** Start of the Middle Kingdom Period of Egyptian history, as Mentuhotep II, ruler of Upper Egypt, conquers Lower Egypt to reunite the country.

WESTERN ASIA

👑 **c.2350** A tablet describing reforms undertaken by King Urukagina of Lagash, decreeing laws protecting citizens' rights, includes the first recorded use of the word "freedom."

📖 **c.2300** The oldest surviving map of a city is carved in stone on a statue of the ruler of the Sumerian city-state of Lagash.

⊕ **c.2200** The Sumerians use a 360-day calendar, with an extra month every eight years to keep in step with the seasons.

✕ **c.2190** The Akkadian Empire collapses following attacks by the Gutian people, a tribe from the Zagros Mountains of Iran.

✕ **c.2120** A ruler of Uruk defeats the Gutians, reestablishing Sumerian control of Mesopotamia.

👑 **c.2100** Ur-Nammu seizes control of Mesopotamia as the founder of the powerful Third Dynasty of Ur.

SOUTH & CENTRAL ASIA

👑 **c.2350** Texts record trade links between Sumerian city-states and sites in the Persian Gulf, where Sumerian agricultural products are traded for timber and precious stones shipped from India.

⊕ **c.2200** Irrigation agriculture, probably learned from the Near East, appears in Central Asia.

EAST ASIA & OCEANIA

⊕ **c.2400** Refined, eggshell-thin black pottery, thrown on a potter's wheel, is produced at Longshan, on China's northeastern coast.

👑 **2333** Traditional date for the foundation of the first Korean kingdom, established by a legendary, semidivine ruler called Tangun.

👑 **c.2200** According to later Chinese histories, a dynasty called the Xia is established in northern China.

2500–2000 B.C.

EGYPT'S OLD KINGDOM

▲ The Palette of Narmer shows Narmer, king of Egypt in about 3000 B.C., smiting an enemy with his war club; other defeated foes lie under his feet. The falcon symbolizes the god Horus, usually shown with a falcon's head; the papyrus reeds on which he perches are the symbols of marshy Lower Egypt.

SEEN FROM SPACE, *the Nile Valley cuts a ragged green slash across an otherwise uninterrupted expanse of desert. It is water that makes the difference: Even in the dry season the Nile never ceases to flow, and it is dramatically swollen by summer rains in the Ethiopian Highlands. Today the river is controlled by hydroelectric dams that provide modern Egypt with much-needed energy; but the dams have also brought to an end a natural cycle that had continued unbroken for countless generations. The annual flood not only watered the Nile Valley but also replenished its fields with rich, river-borne soils. In so doing, it allowed overworked lands to renew themselves, creating the necessary conditions for the development of one of the world's longest-lasting civilizations.*

By 4000 B.C. agriculture in the Nile Valley was so productive that it could support a significant nonfarming population. It was concentrated in small urban clusters like the one excavated at Naqada, just downriver from modern Luxor (formerly Thebes). Prosperous though these communites were, however, their neighbors had as yet no need to envy them: Climate change was only just starting to set the lush Nile Valley apart in an increasingly arid region. The trend was irreversible, though, and an emergent Egypt gathered impetus from this wider crisis.

⊛ **c.6000 B.C.** Hunter-gatherers start turning to settled agriculture along the Nile Valley.

⊛ **c.4000** At Naqada, near modern Luxor, a simple village culture flourishes.

⊛ **c.3500** Rectangular brick houses replace circular huts at Naqada and other sites. Walled towns appear.

⊛ **c.3500** Desertification of the Sahara intensifies.

⊛ **c.3300** By this date Egyptians are using both river- and ocean-going sailing boats.

⊛ **c.3200** The first known examples of hieroglyphic writing date from about this time.

👑 **c.3100** Upper (upstream, or southern) and Lower (northern) Egypt are united under the kings of the Predynastic Period.

👑 **c.3000** Narmer, the best-known of the Predynastic kings, rules a united Egypt from the city of Abydos.

👑 **c.2950** Egypt's Early Dynastic Period begins when the First Dynasty is established under the Pharaoh Menes.

⊛ **c.2650** Djoser's Step Pyramid is built.

👑 **c.2575** The Fourth Dynasty gets under way as Sneferu succeeds Huni as pharaoh.

⊛ **c.2550** Work begins on the Great Pyramid, built at Giza (on the outskirts of modern Cairo) for the Pharaoh Khufu.

👑 **c.2450** Userkaf comes to power, inaugurating the Fifth Dynasty.

👑 **c.2325** The reign of Teti introduces Egypt's Sixth Dynasty.

👑 **c.2250** Reign of Pepi II begins.

👑 **c.2200** Drought throughout northeast Africa leads to famine along the Nile and prompts persistent raiding by increasingly desperate desert nomads.

👑 **c.2170** Pepi II's increasingly troubled reign ends with his death; his successors fail to maintain pharaonic authority over a disintegrating state.

👑 **c.2125** The Old Kingdom gives way to a time of troubles called by modern scholars the "First Intermediate Period."

Around 3100 B.C. Egypt's various centers came together as a single state whose rulers, the pharaohs, controlled the whole valley from the First Cataract (rapids) of Upper Egypt down to the delta. They did so by means of a powerful mystique: The pharaoh was seen as a god, the provider of the flood and its fertility, and the protector of his people in this life and the next. Hence the importance of the "mortuary cult"— the construction of lavish tombs was not just the religious focus but the economic engine of Egyptian life.

The ordinary Egyptian owed everything to his pharaoh and paid not only in produce but in labor on public works, from palaces and temples to irrigation projects. A vast civil service of scribes administered the whole complicated system, recording everything in their hieroglyphic (picture-based) script. The pharaoh's bureaucracy loomed large in the lives of ordinary Egyptians, but it was this organizational spirit that made possible the development of city life and great works like the pyramids.

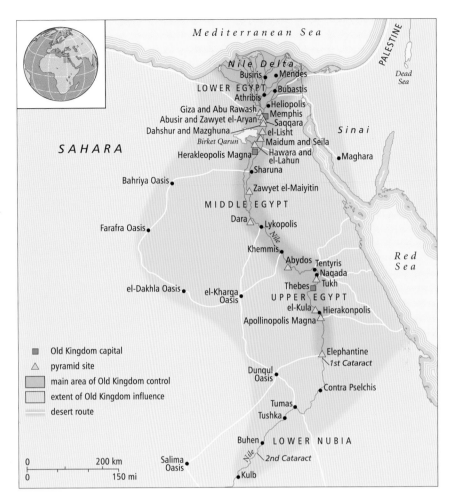

◀ The wealth of ancient Egypt was built on agriculture, which flourished in the rich soil of the Nile Valley. The river was also the nation's main highway; most heavy goods, including the stones for the pyramids, were transported by boat.

▶ Ancient Egypt grew up around the Nile, which formed a ribbon of life in the surrounding desert. The nation was born when the two separate kingdoms of Upper and Lower Egypt united under a single ruler from about 3100 B.C. on.

The Pyramids

At the beginning of the Old Kingdom Period, leading Egyptians were buried in flat-roofed mud-brick tombs known as mastabas. When the first pyramid, that of the Pharaoh Djoser, was built in about 2650 B.C., it took the form of a number of mastabas piled one on top of another, each slightly smaller than the one below. The stepped result offered the departed pharaoh a convenient staircase toward the sun, seen as the source of life. Shortly afterward pyramids began to be built with the familiar straight edges, intended to represent the rays of Ra, the sun god. The first such was also the most impressive: Khufu's Great Pyramid at Giza is still a spectacular sight, towering above the high-rise apartment blocks of the nearby Cairo suburbs. No taller building would be built until the Eiffel Tower in 1889; the pyramid contains a staggering 6 million tons of stone.

17

2000–1500 B.C.

AMERICAS

c.2000 Copper mined in the Great Lakes region is traded and made into tools and ornaments.

c.2000 The nomadic hunter-gatherer groups of North America's Archaic period are increasingly forming settlements, domesticating plants and animals, and cultivating crops.

c.2000 In Central America too, nomads are settling down to a farming life, with ground cornmeal as a staple of their diet.

c. 2000 The Initial Period of South American culture begins in Peru, marked by the introduction of pottery and the spread of agriculture.

c.1800 Coastal villagers in Peru start to build ceremonial complexes featuring large mounds with flattened tops, arranged in a U-shape.

c.1750 A temple is built at La Florida, in Peru's Rimac Valley, and large-scale irrigation projects are undertaken nearby.

EUROPE

c.2000 Minoan civilization enters a new, more splendid phase with the construction of the first palace at Knossos, Crete.

Octopus flask from Minoan Crete.

c.1700 Amber and other luxury items, as well as raw materials like copper and tin, are traded back and forth across central Europe.

AFRICA

c.1897 Senusret II becomes Egypt's pharaoh: He presides over an ambitious reorganization and extension of the country's irrigation system, with dramatic consequences for agricultural production.

c.1878 Senusret III is pharaoh in Egypt: In his 35-year reign he launches a series of military campaigns in Nubia that extend Egypt's frontier southward.

c.1640 Egypt's Middle Kingdom comes to an end as the Hyksos, a loose assemblage of nomadic warriors from the Mediterranean's east coast, take power in northern Egypt. They bring with them the horse-drawn war chariot.

WESTERN ASIA

c.2000 Ironworking spreads across western Asia, although another millennium will pass before the metal is widely available.

c.1950 Elamites from southwest Iran seize Ur, bringing the city's 3rd Dynasty and the great age of Sumerian civilization to an end.

c.1900 The Amorites—Semitic cattle-herders—establish a dynasty of kings in the previously unimportant town of Babylon.

c.1850 The patriarch Abraham, father and founder of the Jewish nation, is believed to have lived in Ur around this time.

c.1792 Hammurabi I comes to the throne as the sixth Amorite king of Babylon. By his death in about 1750 the city is the center of an empire stretching to Assyria and the Zagros Mountains of Iran.

SOUTH & CENTRAL ASIA

c.2000 The Aryan peoples begin their expansion from a homeland somewhere on the steppeland near the Caspian Sea.

c.1900 Having reached its peak around the turn of the millennium, India's Harappan civilization starts to decline.

EAST ASIA & OCEANIA

c.2000 The Ban Kao Culture develops in southern Thailand, producing sophisticated stone tools and a distinctive type of tripod-supported pottery.

c.2000 Rice is cultivated by the Phung Nyugen Culture of northern Vietnam's Red River Valley.

Stele of Hammurabi receiving the Law from the sun god Shamash.

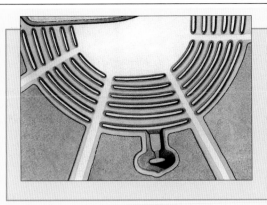

The earthworks at Poverty Point, Louisiana, are among the earliest in North America. The site's main feature is a set of six concentric ridges, over half a mile (1.2 km) across at their widest, that once joined to form a circle, although the eastern half has since eroded away. The ridges may have served to support mud and thatch houses, raising them out of the reach of flooding.

⊕ **c.1600** The Poverty Point Culture, so called after an elaborate mound complex, emerges in Louisiana. Fine tools and jewelry are created in clay, stone, and flint, and there is evidence of trade in copper, lead, and soapstone.

AMERICAS

✕ **c.1700** Palaces at Knossos and Phaistos in Crete are destroyed, probably by earthquake. New palaces soon rise from their ashes.

👑 **c.1600** The Mycenaean civilization emerges on the Greek mainland at about this time.

⊕ **c.1500** Huge trilithons—upright stones supporting a horizontal keystone—are erected at Stonehenge, completing the monument's construction.

EUROPE

👑 **c.1550** Ahmose reunites Egypt and establishes the 18th Dynasty, bringing the Second Intermediate Period to an end and ushering in the New Kingdom.

☀ **c.1504** On his death Amenhotep I becomes the first pharaoh to be buried in the Valley of Kings, a secluded area across the Nile from the capital, Thebes.

✕ **c.1504** Amenhotep is succeeded by Thutmose I, a warrior pharaoh who will lead Egyptian armies against Nubia, then into Palestine and Syria.

AFRICA

📖 **c.1750** The earliest literary classic— the *Epic of Gilgamesh*—is written down.

⊕ **c.1700** Horses come into use as draft animals, revolutionizing transportation. Horseback riding, however, remains uncommon.

👑 **c.1650** The Hittites begin building an empire around their fortified capital at Hattusas in northern Anatolia (modern-day Turkey).

✕ **c.1595** The Hittites under Mursilis I sack Babylon, bringing its power to an end for almost a millennium.

👑 **c.1550** The Mesopotamian city of Mittani, previously obscure, begins an extraordinary rise to fame, taking territories from the Egyptians and the Hittites.

WESTERN ASIA

⊕ **c.1800** Aryans arrive in northwestern India, bringing with them chariots, cattle, and the Sanskrit language.

👑 **c.1750** For reasons that remain unexplained the Indus Valley cities are abandoned by their inhabitants around this time.

SOUTH & CENTRAL ASIA

👑 **c.2000** Austronesians, probably from the Southeast Asian mainland, arrive on New Guinea, already inhabited by Aborigines for more than 20,000 years.

👑 **1766** Traditional date for the foundation of China's Shang Dynasty—the first for which solid archaeological evidence exists.

👑 **c.1650** The Aryan emigration reaches China.

EAST ASIA & OCEANIA

2000–1500 B.C.

THE INDUS VALLEY CIVILIZATION

IN THE EARLY 1920S *British archaeologists investigated two ancient mounds in the Indus Valley region of what is now Pakistan, one close to the village of Mohenjo-Daro and the other at a place called Harappa. To their amazement, at both sites they found the buried remains of large cities lying close to the dried-up courses of old rivers. Excavations subsequently turned up impressive mud-brick city walls, large public buildings, and streets laid out on a regular grid pattern.*

▲ This soapstone bust, just 7 inches (18 cm) high, was found in a small house in the ruins of Mohenjo-Daro. No one knows for sure who it represents, but the figure's ceremonial garb and air of authority have led the sculpture to be commonly known as the "Priest King."

The discovery of these cities was the first indication that a major civilization—known today as the Indus Valley or Harappan civilization—had arisen in the Indian subcontinent more than 4,000 years ago. Archaeologists now believe that the culture first emerged in about 2600 B.C. and lasted until about 1750 B.C. They estimate that Mohenjo-Daro and Harappa had populations of between 30,000 and 40,000—as large as, if not larger than, the cities of Mesopotamia at the same period.

Archaeologists have now uncovered hundreds of towns and villages belonging to the Indus Valley civilization spread over an area of around 260,000 square miles (680,000 sq. km). Buildings were almost invariably constructed of baked brick made to a standard size throughout the region. At Lothal, on the coast, archaeologists have discovered a deepwater dock built entirely of brick.

Brick was also used to build embankments that protected the citadels—the areas where the main public buildings lay—from flooding. As a further precaution they were constructed on flattened earth mounds, raising them safely above the floodplain.

The people in the towns were skilled craftworkers. They made jewelry of polished shell and semiprecious stones, pottery, and copper tools and ornaments, and traded these goods as far as the Persian Gulf and Mesopotamia. Pottery toys found at many sites show that they had wheeled carts and sailed flat-bottomed boats much like those in use on the Indus River today. Their stone seals (probably used as identification tags) were carved with animals such as elephants, rhinos, and oxen. Many seals have writing on them, but scholars are unable to read the pictographic script.

Archaeologists once thought that outside invaders brought the Indus civilization to a violent end. But it now seems rather to have declined gradually, probably during a period of climate warming when the rivers dried up. People abandoned the cities, and writing and craft production fell gradually into disuse, although life in the countryside continued largely unchanged for several centuries more.

Cities of Equals

A striking feature of the Indus Valley cities is that they contained neither palaces nor large monuments similar to the pyramids of ancient Egypt and no rich burial sites like the Royal Cemetery at Ur. From this fact archaeologists conclude that the civilization lacked a ruling elite (privileged class). The cities were usually divided into separate public and residential sectors. The public buildings were located in the upper part of the city (sometimes called the citadel). At Mohenjo-Daro (*right*) the main public building was the Great Bath, probably used for ritual washing. The houses in the residential area, or lower city, were often several stories high and were laid out around courtyards. Most had a well, a brick-paved bathroom, underground drains, and a lavatory.

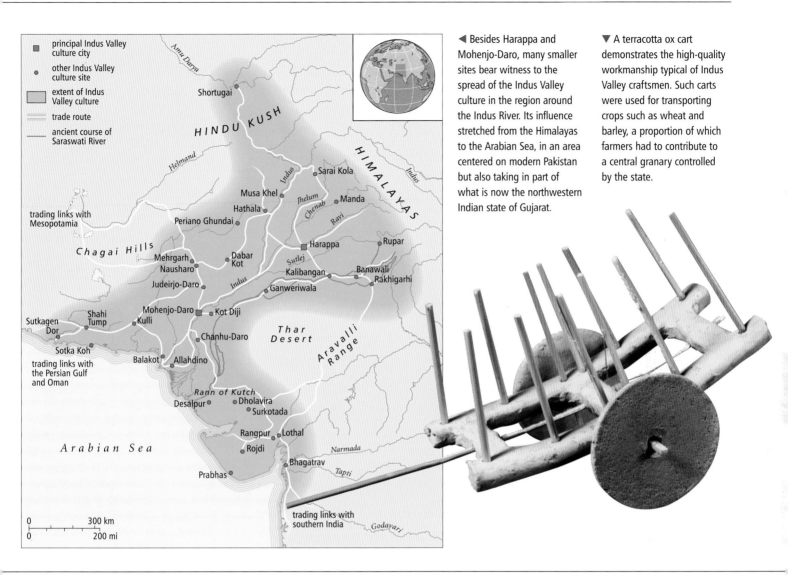

principal Indus Valley culture city

other Indus Valley culture site

extent of Indus Valley culture

trade route

ancient course of Saraswati River

trading links with Mesopotamia

trading links with the Persian Gulf and Oman

trading links with southern India

◀ Besides Harappa and Mohenjo-Daro, many smaller sites bear witness to the spread of the Indus Valley culture in the region around the Indus River. Its influence stretched from the Himalayas to the Arabian Sea, in an area centered on modern Pakistan but also taking in part of what is now the northwestern Indian state of Gujarat.

▼ A terracotta ox cart demonstrates the high-quality workmanship typical of Indus Valley craftsmen. Such carts were used for transporting crops such as wheat and barley, a proportion of which farmers had to contribute to a central granary controlled by the state.

⊕ **c.6500 B.C.** Sheep and goats are farmed at Mehrgarh in the mountains on the northern edge of the Indus Valley.

⊕ **c.4000** Humped cattle (zebu) are by now the most common domesticated animal; wheat and barley are being cultivated.

⊕ **c.4000** Farmers begin to settle on the Indus floodplain and to construct dams and canals for irrigation.

⊕ **c.4000** Copper is in use in the Indus region.

⊕ **c.3500** The potter's wheel is introduced to the Indus region.

⊕ **c.2600** Cities emerge in the Indus Valley.

📖 **c.2350** A reference in a Sumerian text to trade with a distant land called "Meluhha" may refer to the Indus Valley civilization.

👑 **c.2300** Indus Valley civilization is at its height and continues to flourish for the next four centuries.

⊕ **c.2000** First evidence of bronze in the Indus region.

👑 **c.1900** The Indus cities begin to decline.

👑 **c.1750** The cities are finally abandoned at about this time.

1500–1000 B.C.

AMERICAS

c.1500 Village society develops in southern Mexico, marking the start of the Preclassical Period of Mayan civilization.

c.1250 The first great Olmec ceremonial center is established at San Lorenzo, in the tropical lowlands of Mexico's Gulf coast.

c.1200 The first signs of a new culture, known as Chavín after its major ceremonial center, appear in the valleys of the Peruvian Andes.

EUROPE

c.1450 Mount Thera erupts on the Aegean island of Santorini, causing widespread devastation. The Minoan civilization of Crete is fatally damaged.

c.1400 Mycenaeans from the Greek mainland conquer Crete, installing their own ruling dynasty and art styles.

c.1250 Greece's Mycenaean civilization collapses at about this time.

AFRICA

c.1473 Hatshepsut becomes Egypt's second female pharaoh.

c.1458 Thutmose III takes power on Hatshepsut's death.

c.1348 Akhenaten establishes a new capital, Akhetaten, dedicated to the worship of the sun's disk.

c.1333 Tutankhamen comes to power in Egypt.

c.1268 Egypt's Ramses II signs one of the earliest surviving treaties with the Hittite King Hattusilis III, sealing it by marrying Hattusilis's daughter.

Portable throne from the boy Pharaoh Tutankhamen's tomb.

WESTERN ASIA

c.1365 King Assur-uballit I comes to power in Assur; under his rule the city becomes the center of a growing Assyrian empire.

c.1360 Scribes in the Canaanite city of Ugarit employ a written script engraved on clay tablets.

c.1350 Suppiluliumas I becomes king of the Hittites, bringing their empire to its height.

c.1279 Hittite and Egyptian forces meet in the Battle of Kadesh in Syria; both sides claim victory, but the conflict ends with the Egyptian army returning home.

c.1250 The raids of the Sea Peoples cause problems for all the region's established states, from the Mediterranean coast to Assyria.

c.1200 The Hittites are defeated and their main cities destroyed by unknown conquerors.

c.1200 The Jews, under the kingship of Joshua, conquer Canaan.

1184 Traditional date of the fall of Troy to Mycenaean forces, as described in Homer's *Iliad*.

c.1150 Elam briefly threatens Assyrian ascendancy in Mesopotamia.

SOUTH & CENTRAL ASIA

c.1500 Rice cultivation reaches the Ganges Valley, opening up for development a large area of previously unproductive land.

c.1500 The Aryan immigration spreads through India. The Brahmin priesthood becomes the apex of a fixed hierarchy of social "castes" (classes).

c.1500 The first Vedas (hymns to the Hindu gods in the Aryan language Sanksrit) date from this time.

EAST ASIA & OCEANIA

c.1500 Bronze is made into weapons, tools, and ornaments in settlements around Dong Dau in Vietnam's Red River Valley.

c.1500 New Guinea's first stone sculptures—bird, animal, and other figures—are made.

c.1400 In China Shang Dynasty oracle bones dating from this time have been found inscribed with a fully developed script.

Lapita pottery with stamped design.

AMERICAS

👑 **c.1100** Large villages spring up in Oaxaca, southern Mexico.

✷ **c.1000** Pottery-making and ceremonial burials take place at Cuello, northern Belize.

EUROPE

✷ **c.1050** Dorian invaders pour westward into Greece from Anatolia (modern Turkey), bringing with them the secrets of ironworking.

👑 **c.1000** Ionian Greeks, displaced by the Dorian advance, settle on the islands of the eastern Aegean and its Asian coast.

AFRICA

👑 **c.1220** The Israelites leave Egypt on the migration known as the Exodus.

✕ **c.1180** Under Ramses III, Egyptian forces defeat the Sea Peoples, a coalition of displaced eastern Mediterranean tribes, in a naval battle in the Nile Delta.

👑 **c.1163** Ramses III, the last of the great New Kingdom pharaohs, dies following an assassination attempt hatched by some of his courtiers.

✕ **c.1070** The New Kingdom comes to an end as civil war divides the nation.

WESTERN ASIA

From the high plains of central Anatolia (modern Turkey) the Hittites created an empire that endured for 450 years, stretching at its peak deep into present-day Iraq and Syria. Their warriors were famous for their skill in maneuvering heavy, three-man war chariots; their craftsmen excelled in producing elaborate vessels like this silver cup in the form of a stag. Hittite power came to an end around 1200 B.C., when their capital was destroyed by unknown assailants—possibly the mysterious Sea Peoples.

👑 **c.1115** Tiglath-Pileser I succeeds to the throne; his 38-year reign restores Assyrian authority.

✕ **c.1100** Nebuchadrezzar I of Babylon defeats the Elamites.

✷ **c.1100** The Phoenicians adopt a phonetic (sound-based) alphabet—a radical departure from the pictographic scripts that have gone before.

SOUTH & CENTRAL ASIA

✷ **c.1300** Finds of distinctive "gray-ware" pottery in northwestern India underline the growing importance of a distinct Indo-Aryan Culture.

✷ **c.1300** Evidence of ironworking appears in the valley of the Ganges.

EAST ASIA & OCEANIA

✷ **c.1300** Lapita pottery, taking its name from the site in the Bismarck Archipelago where it was originally excavated, makes its first appearance. Its makers will go on to populate Melanesia.

👑 **c.1300** Taking its name from its capital city, located north of China's Yellow River, the Anyang, or Late, Period of the Shang Dynasty gets underway.

✕ **c.1027** The Shang state is overthrown by the neighboring Kingdom of Zhou. The new dynasty extends the cultural advances made in the Shang centuries.

👑 **c.1100** Lapita people reach Fiji, Melanesia's eastern outpost.

👑 **c.1000** Colonists, probably from the Philippines, start to settle Micronesia from this time.

1500–1000 B.C.

NEW KINGDOM EGYPT

ANCIENT EGYPT REACHED THE HEIGHT *of its power and its magnificence in the New Kingdom period, from about 1550 to 1075 B.C. At its peak in the 13th century B.C. the pharaoh's power spread northward up the Mediterranean coast as far as Syria and southward deep into Nubia. The wealth that came from trade and conquest went to build great temples and palaces, as well as the magnificent royal tombs uncovered by archaeologists in the Valley of the Kings outside the capital, Thebes.*

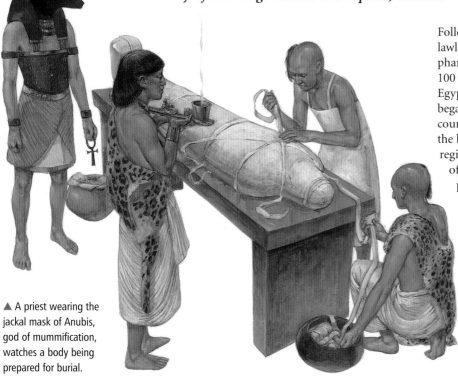

▲ A priest wearing the jackal mask of Anubis, god of mummification, watches a body being prepared for burial.

Following the collapse of the Old Kingdom and the lawlessness of the First Intermediate Period, the pharaohs' authority was restored after a gap of almost 100 years by a fresh royal dynasty, the eleventh since Egypt's history had begun. The Middle Kingdom began when Mentuhotep II managed to reunite the country under his sole rule. Succeeding reigns saw the bureaucracy growing ever more important, regimenting and rationalizing just about every aspect of Egyptian life. The greatest monuments of this period were not imposing royal tombs (although there were some of those) but rather ambitious irrigation projects, which brought extensive areas under cultivation for the first time. Fortresses were also built, notably at Buhen in the south to protected the frontier with Nubia, in what is now the Sudan.

In time the Middle Kingdom's wealth attracted the envy of outsiders. In about 1640 B.C. warriors known as the Hyksos swept into the Nile Delta. They came from the eastern shores of the Mediterranean, and they were equipped with a revolutionary new weapon, the

---

👑 **c.2040 B.C.** Mentuhotep II reunites Egypt, and the Middle Kingdom begins.

👑 **c.1991** Amenemhet I and his 12th Dynasty expand Egyptian territories southward into Nubia.

✳️ **c.1897** Senusret II's reign begins, a time of great achievement for Egypt, with major irrigation projects and other public works.

👑 **c.1640** The Second Intermediate Period begins as a dynasty of Hyksos kings supplants the pharaohs of the 13th Dynasty in the Nile Delta region.

👑 **c.1550** Ahmose comes to power, driving out the Hyksos and inaugurating the 18th Dynasty and the New Kingdom. He goes on to bring much of Palestine and Syria under Egyptian rule.

👑 **c.1473** Queen Hatshepsut comes to power.

👑 **c.1350** Amenhotep IV takes the name Akhenaten and starts a religious revolution focused on worship of the aten, or sun's disk.

👑 **c.1333** The boy-king Tutankhamen succeeds to the throne. Worship of the old gods is restored.

👑 **c.1307** Ramses I ascends the throne, to be followed by the Ramessid rulers of the 19th and 20th dynasties.

👑 **c.1290** Accession of Ramses II, the Great, whose 66-year reign marks the peak of Egyptian power.

⚔️ **c.1285** Ramses II's invasion of Syria is fought to a standstill by the Hittites at the Battle of Kadesh.

👑 **c.1163** The death of Ramses III marks the beginning of the end for New Kingdom Egypt: his successors rule over an empire in decline.

◀ This gold funerary mask was one of the amazing finds from the tomb of Tutankhamen, a boy-pharaoh who ruled Egypt briefly at its New Kingdom peak in the 14th century B.C.

▼ Under a succession of warrior pharaohs New Kingdom Egypt extended its rule far up the Mediterranean's east coast and southward deep into Nubia (today's northern Sudan).

horse-drawn war chariot. The pharaohs were driven out of the delta, but managed to hold on to power in the south, ruling Upper Egypt (the southern half of the country) from Thebes, about 600 miles (1,000 km) upriver.

There, after almost a century had passed, a strong leader, Ahmose, arose to drive out the Hyksos. The interlopers were expelled around the year 1550, bringing Egypt's Second Intermediate Period to an end and ushering in the New Kingdom. Over the next three centuries a succession of warlike pharaohs went on the offensive, striking north up the Mediterranean coast and south into Nubia. For the first time in its history Egypt built up a sizable foreign empire. With military power came economic might. The next few centuries saw Egyptian civilization at its height, with stupendous achievements in art and architecture, medicine, science, and engineering.

The golden age continued until about 1150, at which point events beyond the nation's borders forced it into slow decline. In a time of general economic disarray a wave of uprooted refugees called the Sea Peoples swept across the Mediterranean. Egypt fought off their attacks but lost its empire, and the trade routes that had assured its wealth were disrupted. As its prosperity declined, its military power weakened. The New Kingdom itself came to an end in about 1070 B.C. with the death of its last ruler, Ramses XI.

Over the ensuing centuries Libyans, Nubians, Persians, and Greeks would all at different times hold power in Egypt, putting dynasties of their own on the pharaoh's throne. The final one was that of the Greek Ptolemies, who ruled for almost 300 years. The last of the Ptolemies was the famous Queen Cleopatra; when she committed suicide in 30 B.C., pharaonic rule came to an end, and Egypt became a province of the Roman Empire.

Map

HITTITE EMPIRE
Carchemish
Ugarit
ASSYRIA
Euphrates
Tigris
Cyprus
Qadesh
Byblos
Damascus
Mediterranean Sea
Megiddo
Syrian Desert
Jerusalem
Amman
Dead Sea
Tanis
Kom el-Hisn
Qantir
LOWER EGYPT
Memphis
Sinai
Timna
Sidmant el-Gebel
Serabit el-Khadim
Bahriya Oasis
Hermopolis Magna
Akhetaten
Farafra Oasis
Lykopolis
MIDDLE EGYPT
el-Dakhla Oasis
Abydos
Thebes
el-Kharga Oasis
Apollinopolis Magna
UPPER EGYPT
Elephantine
SAHARA
Aniba
Contra Pselchis
Abu Simbel
Buhen
LOWER NUBIA
Semna
Kumma
Red Sea
Soleb
UPPER NUBIA
Napata
Kerkis
Sanam

Legend:
■ New Kingdom capital
Thebes site with royal tomb of New Kingdom
○ site of temple or chapel
maximum extent of New Kingdom c.1500 B.C.

0   400 km
0   300 mi

The Heretic Pharaoh

The most revolutionary pharaoh in Egypt's history was Amenhotep IV (c.1353–1336), who changed his name to Akhenaten (*right*). Coming to the throne when the New Kingdom was at its height, he made the momentous decision to abandon the worship of the country's many gods and to replace them with a single deity: Aten, the sun's disk. To distance his court from the high priests of the old faith, he moved the capital from Thebes to a new city built in the desert, Akhetaten. There he patronized a fresh style of art, more realistic than the stylized sculpture of earlier times. After his death all his reforms came to nothing. The old gods were restored, the capital was moved back to Thebes, and his successors did all in their power to erase his memory from the historical record.

1000–900 B.C.

AMERICAS

c.1000 The Adena, a North American community of hunter-gatherers also practicing some cultivation, may have begun to develop their culture in southern Ohio at this time (although some authorities favor a later date). They build large earthworks and burial mounds, and hammer artifacts from imported copper.

c.1000 Large-scale societies begin to develop in the southern Andes.

c.1000 The Maya people begin to settle the Yucatán Peninsula.

c.1000 Corn is cultivated in Peru.

c.1000 Olmec civilization spreads from Mexico to parts of Guatemala, Honduras, and Costa Rica. Trade goods include stone, clay, and jade artifacts.

EUROPE

c.1000 The earliest hill-fort sites are constructed in Europe at about this time.

c.1000 Metal craftsmanship employing bronze and copper reaches a high level in Scandinavia.

Bronze and gold sun chariot, from Trundholm in Denmark.

AFRICA

c.950 Rice is domesticated by West African farmers in the flood basins of the middle Niger River.

c.945 Shoshenq I seizes the Egyptian throne, founding a dynasty that endures for over 200 years.

c.924 Shoshenq I invades Israel and Judah.

WESTERN ASIA

c.1000 The Phoenicians, based on the Mediterranean's eastern coast, set up their first overseas trading posts at about this time.

c.1000 Migrating Aryans (Indo-Europeans) form the kingdoms of Media and Parsa (Persia).

c.1000 Arameans from the Syrian desert lands overrun much of Assyria.

Coin from Sidon showing a Phoenician galley.

c.1000 Ironworking techniques spread from the Middle East to southern Europe.

c.1000 King David of Israel captures the fortress city of the Jebusites and renames it Jerusalem.

c.1000 The Phrygian Empire, which originated in Europe two centuries earlier, reaches its widest extent as the Phrygians occupy the central plateau and western edge of Asia Minor.

SOUTH & CENTRAL ASIA

c.1000 The peoples of the Central Asian steppes develop the skills of horseback riding.

c.1000 The later Vedic Age age begins in India; the Brahmanic caste system becomes well established.

c.1000 In southern India the so-called Megalithic Culture develops, marked by stone monuments and burial sites built in circles of stones.

EAST ASIA & OCEANIA

c.1000 Samoa and Tonga in the South Pacific are colonized by Lapita settlers from the eastern islands of Southeast Asia.

c.1000 Skilled bronzemaking is widespread in China.

c.1000 Polynesian Culture develops on the islands of Fiji, Tonga, and Samoa.

☀ **c.1000** By this date Chavín Culture spreads as far as the southern coast of Peru. Its artworks are distinguished by characteristic figures known as the Smiling God and the Staff God.

Chavín Culture, taking its name from a temple at Chavín de Huantar on the Andes' eastern slopes, was the first to spread across all Peru, setting a style whose influence lingered up to Inca times. Its artwork, expressed in stone, gold, and textiles (as in this fabric image of a fanged god), was highly stylized, serving the religious needs of a powerful priestly class.

AMERICAS

⊛ **c.1000** The Vestini tribe of Italy erects an elaborate array of standing stones at Fossa over the next two centuries.

✕ **c.1000** Germanic tribes begin pushing southward into Celtic territory, forcing the Celts to begin a series of warlike migrations into Italy and Greece.

⊛ **c.950** A settlement is founded near salt mines at Hallstatt (in what is now Austria) that will become the center of a widespread Celtic culture.

EUROPE

⊛ **c.920** Tombs at el-Kurru in the Sudan dating from this time indicate the growing wealth of Nubia.

AFRICA

✕ **c.1000** The Chaldeans of southern Babylonia occupy the ancient Sumerian city of Ur.

🎖 **c.969** Hiram I becomes king of Phoenician Byblos, building a harbor at Tyre, his new capital.

🎖 **c.965** Solomon succeeds David as king of Israel; he funds his luxurious court and lavish construction projects by imposing high taxes on his subjects.

☀ **c.950** Solomon builds the Great Temple at Jerusalem.

🎖 **c.935** Assurdan II comes to the throne of Assyria, starting a revival in that nation's fortunes.

🎖 **c.928** Solomon's son Rehoboam becomes king of Israel, but he antagonizes the northern tribes by his uncompromising stance.

🎖 **c.925** The Jewish kingdom separates into the northern kingdom of Israel and the southern kingdom of Judah.

✕ **c.911** Adad-Nirari II becomes king of Assyria; his armies conquer Babylon and defeat the Aramaeans and the people of Urartu, from what is now eastern Turkey.

WESTERN ASIA

✕ **c.950** The war celebrated in India's national epic, the *Mahabharata*, was probably fought at this time.

⊛ **c.900** Steppe horsemen introduce the saddle and horseback archery.

SOUTH & CENTRAL ASIA

🎖 **c.950** In China King Mu, remembered in later legends as a world traveler, dies.

EAST ASIA & OCEANIA

1000–900 B.C.

THE KINGDOM OF ISRAEL

I N COMPARISON TO OTHER ANCIENT EMPIRES *the Israelite kingdom was small and short-lived, but its foundation would resonate through history. The homeland of Israel became a powerful spiritual and political symbol for Jewish people, sustaining them through the centuries of exile and dispersion that followed the kingdom's collapse.*

The Bible describes how Moses led the Israelites out of captivity in pharaonic Egypt to the "promised land" of Canaan, between the Jordan River and the Mediterranean Sea. There they lived in tribes, which were united under their first king, Saul, who reigned from about 1020 to 1006 B.C. David (1006–965) was Israel's next "beloved" king. He conquered the city of Jebus (Jerusalem) and made it the Israelites' center of political power and worship, installing the precious Ark of the Covenant there.

In Jerusalem David's son Solomon (965–928) built a magnificent temple, cedar paneled and richly decorated with bronze and gold. To pay for this and other projects, the king taxed his people heavily, and his son Rehoboam continued the practice. Resenting the burden, the northern tribes split away from the southern kingdom of Judah, forming a separate Jewish kingdom called Israel.

Meanwhile the Assyrians, a Mesopotamian people from the Tigris Valley, began to threaten the other powers in the region. Aided by technological developments such as siege engines and mail armor, the Assyrians were formidable fighters. Internal

🜲 **c.1220 B.C.** Hebrew people (Israelites) begin settling in Canaan.

🜲 **c.1150** Israelites live in tribes led by elders referred to as "judges."

🜲 **c.1020** Saul becomes the first Israelite king.

🜲 **c.1006** David rules first over the southern kingdom of Judah and later over all Israel, establishing his capital at Jerusalem.

🜲 **c.965** Solomon comes to the throne, presiding over a splendid court; to pay for its expense, he exacts high taxes from the Israelites.

☀ **c.950** King Solomon builds the Temple in Jerusalem.

🜲 **c.930** The Assyrian Empire becomes dominant in the Tigris Valley region.

🜲 **c.928** Solomon's son Rehoboam becomes king, but antagonizes the northern tribes: "My father chastised you with whips," he tells them, "but I will chastise you with scorpions."

✕ **c.925** The northern tribes rebel, splitting away from the southern kingdom of Judah to set up a separate, northern kingdom of Israel.

✕ **c.924** Shoshenq I of Egypt invades Judah and Israel.

✕ **c.854** Israel joins forces with other states to check Assyrian progress at the Battle of Karkar.

🜲 **c.841** Israel is forced to pay tribute (a payment acknowledging submission) to Assyria.

✕ **c.732** Tiglath-Pileser III of Assyria conquers Damascus. Over the next 17 years the Assyrians also overcome Babylon and make Israel and Judah vassal (subject) states.

✕ **c.724** Hoshea, king of Israel, rebels against Assyrian rule.

✕ **c.721** Samaria, the capital of Israel, is captured by the Assyrians after a three-year siege; its inhabitants are deported to Assyria.

🜲 **612** The Assyrian Empire breaks down.

discord had weakened Israel, which was conquered by the Assyrians in 721.

The southern Jewish kingdom of Judah survived the defeat as a vassal (subject) state of the great empire of Babylon, another Mesopotamian power. When the people of Judah revolted against Babylonian rule in 598, the Babylonian king, Nebuchadrezzar II (604–562), known in the Bible as Nebuchadnezzar, crushed the uprising. Ten years later, after another rebellion, he besieged Jerusalem, destroying the city and temple and deporting thousands of Jews to Babylon.

Babylon was a magnificent city, famed for its Hanging Gardens, but the Babylonian Captivity was harsh for the exiles. Accordingly, they welcomed Babylon's overthrow in 539 by the Persians, who had risen to greatness under Cyrus the Great (died 530). As the new ruler of Babylon, Cyrus encouraged the exiled Jews to return to their own land, which now also formed part of his empire. Many went home, but thousands remained in Babylon or in Egypt, beginning the dispersion, or "diaspora," of the Jewish people that continued into modern times.

◀ As described in the biblical Book of Kings, the temple that Solomon built in Jerusalem to house the Ark of the Covenant consisted of three rooms: an outer porch or vestibule, an inner place of worship, and the Holy of Holies, where the Ark rested.

▶ Israel reached its greatest extent in the reign of David, but shrank back after his death. In about 925 B.C. the remaining lands split into two separate states: Israel in the north, with its capital at Samaria, and Judah in the south, ruled from Jerusalem.

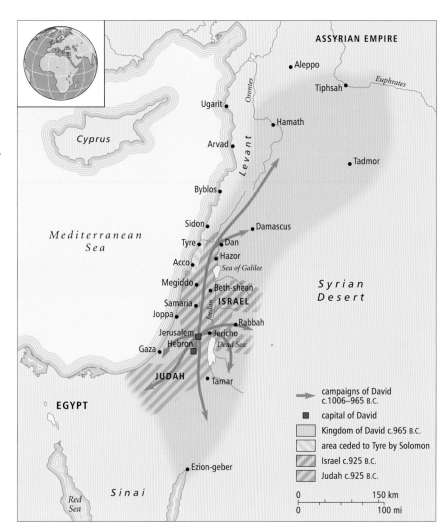

→ campaigns of David c.1006–965 B.C.

■ capital of David

Kingdom of David c.965 B.C.

area ceded to Tyre by Solomon

Israel c.925 B.C.

Judah c.925 B.C.

0   150 km
0   100 mi

The Ark of the Covenant

The Ark of the Covenant was a box of acacia wood and gold, topped with two sculpted cherubs and carried on two long poles; the Bible relates that God instructed Moses to have it made to store the tablets listing the Ten Commandments. When the Israelites went to war, the ark was always carried with their soldiers; it served as a focal point for worship and was also believed to have the power to kill people. King David brought the ark to Jerusalem, where it was eventually housed in the temple built by his son, Solomon. But when the Babylonians captured Jerusalem and destroyed the temple in 586 B.C., the ark disappeared. Although the fictional Indiana Jones was able to track it down in the 1981 film *Raiders of the Lost Ark*, its real-life whereabouts remain a mystery.

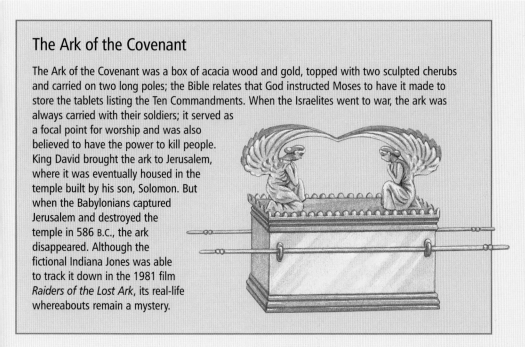

👑 **609–605** Judah comes under Egyptian control.

👑 **c.600** The Neo-Babylonian Empire is established.

⚔ **586** Jerusalem, capital of Judah, is destroyed after a long siege by the Babylonian ruler Nebuchadrezzar II; its inhabitants are deported to Babylon.

👑 **539** Cyrus the Great takes over from the Chaldeans as ruler of Babylon and allows exiled Jews to return to their homeland.

☀ **c.515** A new temple is completed in the rebuilt Jerusalem.

29

AMERICAS

⊛ **c.900** The Chorreran Culture flourishes in Ecuador; among its fine pottery products are distinctive "whistle bottles," which produce a whistling sound when liquid is poured into them.

✕ **c.900** The Olmec ceremonial center at San Lorenzo in Mexico is destroyed, and the monumental stone heads that adorned it are ritually defaced and buried in piled-earth ridges.

⊛ **c.900** A phase of intense cultural activity in the Valley of Mexico, marked by the extraordinary pottery produced at Tlatilco near modern Mexico City, comes to an end, leaving the central Mexican region as something of a cultural backwater for several centuries to come.

☀ **c.900** The great ceremonial center at Chavín de Huantar in Peru is built from about this time on.

EUROPE

♛ **c.900** Sparta is founded in the southern Peloponnese region of Greece; its citizens become renowned for their military discipline and austere lifestyle.

Villanovan hut-shaped burial urn.

⊛ **c.900** The Villanova Culture emerges in the Bologna region of Italy; Villanovan society is notable for its bronzeworking and early use of iron.

AFRICA

♛ **c.900** The state of Kush emerges in Nubia, south of Egypt, with its capital at Napata.

♛ **c.817** Under the 23rd Dynasty Egypt breaks up into rival power centers.

♛ **c.814** The Phoenician colony of Carthage is founded in North Africa.

WESTERN ASIA

📖 **c.900** The people of the kingdom of Urartu, based around Lake Van in what is now eastern Turkey, adopt the Assyrian cuneiform script.

♛ **c.900** Phoenician colonists continue their westward expansion, founding settlements near metal deposits.

♛ **c.883** Assurnarsipal II ascends the throne of Assyria, further expanding the empire into Syria as far as the Mediterranean Sea.

The homeland of the Phoenicians was a narrow strip of the eastern Mediterranean shoreline in what is now Lebanon. Their only outlet for expansion was by sea, and from about 1000 B.C. on, they became famous as traders and voyagers, traveling even beyond the Straits of Gibraltar to explore the western coasts of Africa and Europe. Trade brought in wealth, which in turn supported skilled craftworkers producing dyed cloth, jewelry, and metalwork. This statuette of a bull, reminiscent of the biblical Golden Calf, is thought to symbolize the Phoenician fertitlity god Baal.

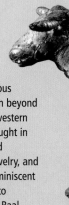

SOUTH & CENTRAL ASIA

☀ **c.900** The later Vedas are composed in India, completing the *Rig Veda*, a collection of 1,028 Hindu hymns that is the world's oldest sacred book.

♛ **c.900** The first states emerge on the Ganges plain in India.

♛ **c.800** Towns are established in India's Ganges Valley.

☀ **c.800** In India the Brahmanas are composed as instructions to priests, designed to provide direction in matters of ritual.

While the Olmec heartland lay near Mexico's Gulf Coast, the Zapotecs came to dominate the Oaxaca Valley region inland from the Pacific Ocean. In its early stages the Zapotec Culture was influenced by the Olmecs, and Zapotec society reflected Olmec models in being ruled by an elite warrior class dedicated to the worship of gods and ancestors. In time, however, the Zapotecs developed a cultural identity of their own; they were the first Americans to devise a written script. Their capital of Monte Albán, shown here, was built from 500 B.C. on.

AMERICAS

📖 **c.850** Olmec cave paintings in southern Mexico depict figures combining human and animal features.

⚙️ **c.800** Numerous villages are established by this date in the tropical lowland regions of Guatemala.

📖 **c.800** Zapotecs—Central American Indians inhabiting southern Mexico—develop a hieroglyphic script that is the earliest in the Americas.

EUROPE

👑 **c.850** Greece begins to emerge from the dark ages that began around 1200 B.C., establishing city-states in Ionia and Aeolia.

👑 **c.850** The first settlements appear on the site of Rome's Palatine Hill.

👑 **c.800** Corinth is founded in the northeastern corner of Greece's Peloponnese Peninsula; it will become the largest and richest Greek city-state after Athens.

👑 **c.800** Athens and Sparta grow in power and grandeur.

⚙️ **c.800** The Celtic Hallstatt Culture spreads out across Europe. Adherents have distinctive burial practices and use bronze and iron tools.

AFRICA

⚙️ **c.800** Ironworking begins to spread across sub-Saharan Africa.

WESTERN ASIA

👑 **c.880** Nimrud, near the present-day city of Mosul in Iraq, becomes the capital of the Assyrian Empire.

👑 **c.876** Phoenicia agrees to pay tribute to the Assyrians.

👑 **c.873** Ahab comes to the throne of Israel.

👑 **c.858** Shalmaneser III ascends the throne of Assyria; the empire expands further during his reign.

✖️ **c.856** Shalmaneser III of Assyria defeats Aramu, the first known king of Urartu.

✖️ **c.854** The Assyrians defeat a coalition of Levantine forces, including Israel, at the Battle of Karkar; despite the victory, their advance is checked.

👑 **c.853** The Babylonian kings become reliant on the military assistance of the Assyrians.

☀️ **c.850** In Israel the prophets Elijah and Elisha attack the cult of the Phoenician god Baal.

👑 **c.850** The Medes migrate from Central Asia to the area southwest of the Caspian Sea.

✖️ **c.842** In Israel Jehu seizes power; King Ahab's widow Jezebel is thrown from a window and crushed to death under the wheels of Jehu's chariot.

👑 **c.841** A weakened Israel is forced to pay tribute to Assyria.

👑 **c.840** The kingdom of Urartu emerges as a significant power in the Middle East.

SOUTH & CENTRAL ASIA

☀️ **c.800** The early Upanishads also date from about this time; a departure from the old Vedic beliefs, these texts represent an attempt to get close to the inner meaning of life.

900–800 B.C.

HOMER'S GREECE

G REECE HAS A UNIQUE PLACE *in Western tradition as the central source of our civilization, yet around the year 2000 B.C. its prospects hardly looked promising. In the Middle East and Egypt great cities had already come and gone; in the valley of the Indus the Harappan civilization was at its height. Greece, however, had only recently shaken off a Stone Age lifestyle as Bronze Age culture had been brought across the Aegean Sea by "island-hopping" immigrants from Anatolia, in what is now Turkey.*

▲ Very little is known of the life of Homer, Greece's great epic poet, but legend claims that he was Ionian—born across the Aegean Sea from mainland Greece—and that he was blind.

▶ From the 11th century B.C. on, when northern Dorians swept into mainland Greece, colonists chose to sail east in search of new homes. They settled on Aegean islands and on the shores of Asia Minor, in what is now Turkey.

⊛ **c.2300 B.C.** Immigrants from Anatolia bring Bronze Age culture to Greece.

⊛ **c.2000** The first Minoan palaces are built in Crete.

☀ **c.1600** The Mycenaean civilization emerges in mainland Greece.

☀ **c.1450** Mt. Thera erupts, causing devastation across the eastern Mediterranean and destroying some cities of Minoan Crete.

☀ **c.1250** Mycenaean civilization collapses.

☀ **1184** Traditional date of the Fall of Troy.

⊛ **c.1050** Dorian nomads invade Greece from the north, bringing with them the secrets of ironworking.

☀ **c.1000** Greek settlers start to establish colonies on the Aegean's eastern coast in regions that will become known as Aeolia and Ionia.

📖 **776** The first Olympic Games.

☀ **c.750** Greece's Archaic Period begins; the first city-states date from this time.

📖 **c.750** The first evidence of a Greek alphabet comes from this period.

📖 **c.750** The great epics of Homer are composed (although not yet written down).

☀ **c.734** The first Greek colonies are founded in Sicily.

📖 **c.700** The poet Hesiod's *Theogony* records traditional stories of the Greek gods.

The first significant civilization of mainland Greece emerged in about 1600 B.C. Its capital lay at Mycenae on the Pelopennese, the peninsula forming the southern part of the Greek mainland. The awe-inspiring ruins excavated there suggest a militaristic culture, yet Mycenae was also a merchant civilization. Soldiers and traders worked together to spread its influence across the eastern Mediterranean region.

The civilization's success was glorious but fleeting: By 1250 B.C. it had collapsed. The reasons for its fall remain unclear. A time of troubles was affecting the eastern Mediterranean, and a mysterious coalition of displaced migrants, known in Egyptian records as the "Sea Peoples," was on the move. Even if they did not destroy Mycenae itself, their activities would certainly have disrupted its seaborne trading network.

Mycenae fell leaving no successor civilization; instead, local warlords fought over a land of scattered settlements. Later scholars talked of the years from 1250 to 850 B.C. as Greece's "Dark Age," although we have no way of knowing how bleak it really was for those who lived through it.

By the 8th century B.C., however, the outlook was certainly brightening. The growing wealth of successful local rulers stimulated craft industries and trade, creating perfect conditions for the evolution of the *polis*, or self-governing city-state, often consisting of little more than one large community and its surrounding countryside. Young adventurers from these cities founded trading posts abroad, enriching their home states even further. While individual cities grew independently, their sense of a common Greek identity was growing too, fostered by a shared set of stories of gods and heroes. Almost nothing is known of the poet Homer (some even suggest "he" was actually more than one anonymous bard), but his great epics, the *Iliad* and the *Odyssey*, became an inspiration to the Greeks of future generations.

Crete's Minoan Civilization

Graceful athleticism triumphed over brute strength in Minoan culture, which flourished from around 2000 B.C. on the Mediterranean island of Crete. This spectacular civilization took its name from the legendary King Minos, whose name also lived on in Greek myths of the Minotaur. This monster lived in a mazelike structure called the Labyrinth, perhaps inspired by tales of the genuinely labyrinthine palace in the Minoan capital, Knossos (*above*). Under royal supervision a trading economy prospered, making commercial connections from pharaonic Egypt to Asia Minor. However, the island's sea-trade empire suffered a fatal blow in about 1450, when Mount Thera, a volcano on the nearby island of Santorini, erupted, devastating much of the eastern Mediterranean region. Political oblivion soon followed; the island was conquered by Mycenaean Greeks by about 1400 B.C.

◀ The palace at Knossos in northern Crete was the focal point of the Minoan civilization that flourished on the island from c.2000 to 1400 B.C. Sprawling across 5 acres (2 hectares) of hilly ground, the many-storied building served not just as a royal residence but also as a statehouse, a religious shrine, a center of craft production, and a warehouse for many different kinds of goods.

▼ Greek legends of youths sacrificed to the monstrous Minotaur—half-man, half-bull—may have been inspired by the real-life Cretan sport of bull leaping. Contestants caught a charging bull by the horns and tried to somersault over its back, as shown in this fresco from the palace at Knossos, dated c.1500 B.C.

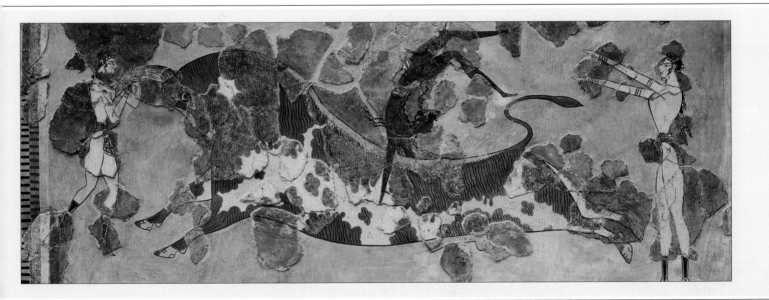

AMERICAS

c.800 The Dorset Culture begins to emerge around Cape Dorset on Canada's Baffin Island; its people display a new grace and precision in the crafting of flint blades and ivory figures.

c.800 The Chavín Culture becomes established through much of the Andean region. Chavín craftsmen produce intricate artworks of hammered gold.

c.800 By this date La Venta, near Mexico's Gulf Coast, has taken the place formerly occupied by San Lorenzo as the main focus of Olmec religious and cultural activity.

EUROPE

c.800 Etruscans establish the first towns in Italy, building on hillside terraces and surrounding their settlements with huge timbered walls.

c.800 The success of Euboea's trading post at Al Mina, on the coast of Syria, starts a trend among other Greek cities for colonization.

776 The first Olympic Games are held at Olympia in southern Greece.

753 The traditional date of the foundation of Rome.

c.750 First use of the Greek alphabet dates from this period: The Greeks use the existing Phoenician letters, but introduce vowels to allow the accurate reproduction of spoken language.

Painted Greek vase of the Archaic Period from Corinth.

AFRICA

c.780 King Kashta's Kush (in what is now Sudan) starts encroaching on the southern territories of a weakened Egypt.

c.770 Kashta takes control of Upper Egypt.

c.750 Kashta's son Piye invades Lower Egypt, making it too subject to Nubia.

WESTERN ASIA

Hebrew captives of the Assyrian King Sennacherib.

c.800 By this date the Phoenician trading empire extends through much of the coastal Mediterranean.

c.760 A weakened Assyria can find no economic or military answer to the rise of Urartu to the north: There are insurrections in several nominally subject cities.

c.744 Tiglath-Pileser III comes to the throne of a much reduced and enfeebled Assyria. He sets about building, by both military and diplomatic means, what will later be known as the "Neo-Assyrian" Empire.

c.738 Midas becomes king of Phrygia in central Anatolia: The legend of his "golden touch" gives some sense of the stupendous wealth of his newly powerful realm.

c.732 Tiglath-Pileser incorporates Damascus into his empire.

c.727 Sargon II seizes the Assyrian throne. In a 16-year reign he defeats both Elam and Urartu, and reimposes Assyrian power over much of the Middle East.

c.721 Assyrian forces take the Israelite capital of Samaria after a three-year siege.

EAST ASIA & OCEANIA

c.800 Wet rice cultivation and bronze technology are exported from China to Korea.

c.800 Rapid urban expansion takes place in China despite increasing lawlessness as the king's power is weakened.

771 King Yu is dethroned and killed by an alliance of rebellious noblemen and steppe nomads.

☀️ **c.750** In the Mayan region of Central America work begins on the ceremonial site at Los Mangales, which will eventually feature temple platforms, tomb complexes, and residential areas.

📖 **c.750** Greek craftsmen increasingly use animal figures rather than geometric patterns in ceramic decoration, showing that they are importing cultural ideas, as well as raw materials, from their Asiatic colonies.

👑 **750** The conventional starting point for the Archaic Period in preclassical Greece.

👑 **c.734** Greeks from Corinth establish the colony of Syracuse in Sicily.

Archaic Greek marble bust of a lady holding a pomegranate.

⚔ **c.716** The Nubian ruler Shabako formally annexes Lower Egypt, thereby officially reuniting the country.

⚔ **c.707** Sargon II conquers Babylon.

👑 **c.705** Sennacherib suceeds to the throne of an Assyrian Empire that is bigger and stronger than it has ever been.

⚔ **c.701** Poised to seize Jerusalem, the all-conquering army of Sennacherib is forced to withdraw for reasons that remain obscure—perhaps an outbreak of plague; the Jews believe they have been saved by their god Yahweh.

⊛ **c.700** Earliest date for construction work at Kaminaljuyú, on the outskirts of modern Guatemala City, which in time will become an important Mayan site.

⚔ **c.730** The Greek city-state of Sparta attacks neighboring Messenia: after a bitter, 20-year war the Messenians' territory is taken and they themselves enslaved.

📖 **c.700** Drawing on preexisting oral traditions, Hesiod's *Theogony* relates the origins and histories of the Greek gods.

For more than seven centuries the Assyrians were among the most feared military powers in the Middle East. From a homeland around the city of Assur on the Tigris River in what is now northern Iraq they spread their influence by conquest, subduing neighboring peoples and demanding tribute from them. At its peak in the 8th century B.C. their empire stretched all the way from the Zagros Mountains of Persia to the Mediterranean coast and into Israel. This bronze image of a charioteer comes from the Balawat Gates, commissioned by Shalmaneser III to celebrate his victories.

👑 **770** Yu's son moves his capital eastward from Hao to Luoyang to distance it further from the steppe nomads. The Eastern Zhou Period gets under way.

👑 **722** The start of the Spring and Autumn Period of Chinese history.

AMERICAS

EUROPE

AFRICA

WESTERN ASIA

EAST ASIA & OCEANIA

800–700 B.C.

THE OLMECS

THE FIRST GREAT CULTURE *of Central America arose in a seemingly unlikely spot—the steamy rainforests of southern Mexico. There, sometime about 1250 B.C., a previously unknown people suddenly started raising spectacular ceremonial centers where previously there had only been scattered villages. Even more surprisingly, they decorated them with huge stone sculptures that still stand comparison with the finest produced anywhere in the world.*

▲ A tiny bust of a woman carved in rare blue jade demonstrates the Olmecs' skill in stone carving. Their sculptors only had stone tools with which to grind and chip the figures into shape.

► From a heartland in the steamy rainforest lands around the Gulf of Mexico, Olmec cultural influence spread out over the course of several centuries through much of Mexico and on into Guatemala, Honduras, and El Salvador.

Olmec ceremonial center
Olmec-influenced site
Olmec heartland
spread of Olmec influence 13th–5th century B.C.

0   250 km
0   175 mi

✱ **c.6500 B.C.**	Chili peppers, cotton, and a variety of squash are cultivated in southern Mexico.	
✱ **c.4000**	Indian corn (maize) first cultivated in Central America.	
✱ **c.3500**	Beans first cultivated in Central America. Semipermanent villages appear, with pit huts replacing the rock shelters used by hunter-gatherers.	
✱ **c.2300**	First pottery made in southern Mexico.	

✱ **c.2000**	By this date agriculture has replaced nomadic (wandering) hunting and gathering as the typical lifestyle in the region.
☀ **c.1400**	First evidence of a raised earthen mound in the Olmec region, from a site on Guatemala's Pacific coast.
☀ **c.1250**	The first great Olmec ceremonial center built at San Lorenzo in the Gulf region of southern Mexico.
☀ **c.1200**	The earliest stone sculptures are erected at San Lorenzo.

✕ **c.900**	San Lorenzo is destroyed, and the great stone statues are defaced and buried.
♔ **c.800**	La Venta, near the Gulf Coast, becomes the main center of Olmec Culture.
✕ **c.400**	La Venta is demolished and its monuments buried.
♔ **c.200**	The ceremonial center of Tres Zapotes falls into disuse, marking the end of the Olmec civilization.

San Lorenzo, the first such center, was built on an earth platform 150 feet (45 m) high—the height of a 10-story building. On this base its builders raised additional earthen mounds arranged in clusters around rectangular courtyards. They decorated the courts with huge sculpted heads, the biggest of them up to 11 feet (3.4 m) tall and weighing as much as 20 tons. The stone from which they were shaped was brought laboriously by raft—the Olmecs had no wheeled vehicles—from mountains 50 miles (80 km) away and carved with stone tools, since their craftsmen had no metals.

Scholars think that the heads probably represented dead rulers. Some are shown wearing helmets rather like those now worn by football players. The connection may not be entirely far-fetched, since the Olmecs are known to have devised a ritual ballgame, played on special courts, that was later passed on to almost all subsequent Central American civilizations. Players of the game, which probably had some ritual significance, were not allowed to touch the ball with their hands or feet; instead, they controlled it with their elbows, hips, and thighs.

To judge from small sculptures, ornaments, and other artifacts found from northern Mexico to El Salvador and Costa Rica, the Olmecs controlled widespread trade networks across Central America.

Apart from small numbers of craftsmen and traders, their society seems to have divided between a wealthy ruling class and the peasant farmers who provided the labor to build the ceremonial centers. Maybe the peasants resented the demands made on them; certainly San Lorenzo was deliberately destroyed around the year 900 B.C., when the monumental heads lining its courts were defaced and buried.

Subsequently, other centers rose to prominence to replace it, first at La Venta on an island in the Tonalá River, and then, when that in turn was overthrown, at Tres Zapotes. That site too seems to have fallen into disuse by about 200 B.C., bringing Olmec civilization to an end.

Yet its influence lived on in later Central American cultures—peoples such as the Maya, the Toltecs, and the Aztecs all borrowed heavily from the Olmecs. The innovations that they passed on to their successors went well beyond the ballgame to also include astronomic calendars, a taste for massive stone architecture, and even a form of pictographic writing.

▼ This colossal stone head is one of 17 found at the ceremonial site of La Venta. All were sculpted from volcanic basalt rock between about 1200 and 900 B.C. The heads range in height from 5 to 11 feet (1.5–3.4 m) and weigh as much as 20 tons. This figure is wearing the headdress that may be associated with the Olmecs' ritual ballgame.

The Jaguar Cult

Olmec sculptures and carvings often depict people whose faces have the slit eyes and snarling mouths of jaguars. Frequently the figure shown is a baby or infant, its forehead imprinted with the stylized image of a big cat's pawmarks. Scholars call these creatures "were-jaguars," after the manner of werewolves, and think that they indicate the existence of a cult devoted to the big cats—the top predators of the Central American jungles. It may be that Olmec nobles traced their origins back to a mythical founder who was himself half-man, half-jaguar, thereby claiming for themselves some of the jaguar's attributes of fierceness and cunning. In one chief's grave the bones of a child have been found buried alongside those of two jaguars, strengthening the idea of a direct link between the animals and nobly born young.

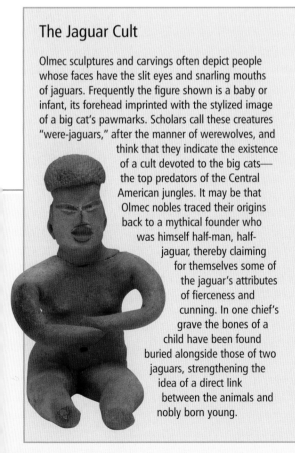

AMERICAS

⊛ **c.700** The Adena Culture is by now firmly established in the Ohio River valley region. Over 200 Adena sites, built over several centuries, have been identified in Ohio and neighboring areas of West Virginia, Pennsylvania, Kentucky, and Indiana.

For more than 1,000 years the building of burial mounds was a central feature of America's eastern woodlands cultures. Ohio's famous Serpent Mound is thought by some experts to be an Adena site (there are others nearby), although others link it to the later Hopewell Culture.

EUROPE

⊛ **c.700** Scandinavian craftsmen exhibit their bronzeworking skills by making lurs—trumpetlike musical instruments probably used in ritual ceremonies.

⊛ **c.700** The peoples of Central Europe build wooden trackways to carry carts over marshy areas.

📖 **c.700** The first known inscriptions in the Etruscan language date from this time.

👑 **683** In Athens, Greece, hereditary kingship comes to an end, to be replaced with elected officials.

👑 **654** The Phoenicians found trading colonies on the Balearic Islands in the western Mediterranean.

👑 **c.650** Tyrants seize power in several Greek city-states in opposition to aristocratic rule (–600).

AFRICA

⚔ **c.671** The Assyrian King Esarhaddon raids Egypt, conquering Memphis and demanding tribute.

⚔ **c.667** Esarhaddon's successor Ashurbanipal defeats Taharqa, the last of the Kushite (Nubian) pharaohs of Egypt.

👑 **c.665** Driven out of Egypt, the Kushites continue to rule most of Nubia from their capital at Napata.

WESTERN ASIA

👑 **c.700** Achaemenes founds the Persian Achaemenid Dynasty.

⊛ **c.700** Babylonian astrologers identify the signs of the zodiac.

📖 **c.690** The Assyrian King Sennacherib rebuilds the ancient capital of Nineveh and decorates the walls of his palace with reliefs of his military victories.

⚔ **689** The Assyrians sack Babylon after the Babylonians rebel against Assyrian rule.

⊛ **673** Babylonian astrologers correctly predict a solar eclipse.

👑 **640** Persia becomes a vassal state of the kingdom of the Medes.

☀ **c.630** The Persian prophet Zoroaster is born.

👑 **626** Nabopolassar, appointed governor of Babylon by the Assyrians, rebels and sets up his own Chaldean dynasty.

👑 **614** Cyaxares, ruler of the Medes, allies himself with Nabopolassar, king of Babylon, against the Assyrians.

⚔ **612** The Assyrian Empire falls to the Medes and Babylonians.

The Ishtar Gate at Babylon, made of blue-glazed bricks.

EAST ASIA & OCEANIA

👑 **c.670** Qi, in the northeast, becomes the dominant state in China during the early Spring and Autumn Period.

👑 **660** According to early Japanese legend, Jimmu becomes the first emperor of Japan.

⊛ **c.600** Iron casting spreads across China from this date.

📖 **c.700** In Central America red-orange pottery of the Mamón style is in use among the Mayan people of the Petèn Lowlands of northern Guatemala.

☀ **c.600** The Middle Formative Period of Mesoamerican culture is now fully under way. In the Mayan lands construction has begun at ceremonial sites including Nakbe, Chalchuapa, Komchen, Rio Azul, and Seibal.

☀ **c.600** The Olmec ceremonial center at Teopantecuanitlán, near Copalillo in the mountains of southwestern Mexico, is abandoned for unknown reasons.

AMERICAS

👑 **c.650** At about this time Perdiccas I is traditionally supposed to have founded the kingdom of Macedon in northern Greece.

👑 **621** The Athenian politician Draco draws up a code of laws that become notorious for their "draconian" severity.

👑 **c.616** A line of Etruscan kings is established in Rome.

📖 **c.600** The poetess Sappho flourishes on the Greek island of Lesbos.

⚙ **c.600** Coinage comes into use on the Greek mainland.

👑 **c.600** Greek colonies are founded at Massilia (modern Marseille) in southern France and at Emporia in southern Spain.

👑 **c.600** Celtic peoples cross the Pyrenees and settle on the Iberian Peninsula.

EUROPE

⚔ **c.651** An Egyptian uprising, led by Psammetichus I, forces the Assyrians to leave Egypt.

⚙ **c.600** Ironworking is known in Kush.

⚙ **c.600** The Egyptian Pharaoh Necho II builds a canal linking the Nile River with the Red Sea.

⚙ **c.600** According to the 5th-century Greek historian Herodotus, Necho also sends a Phoenician fleet to sail around Africa, a voyage that takes three years.

AFRICA

👑 **604** Nebuchadrezzar II becomes king of Babylon and revives its fortunes; his empire is known to historians as the Neo-Babylonian Empire.

📖 **c.600** The Scythians, nomadic herders of Central Asia, begin making gold objects in the "animal style," depicting leaping animals such as deer, horses, and eagles in intertwining patterns.

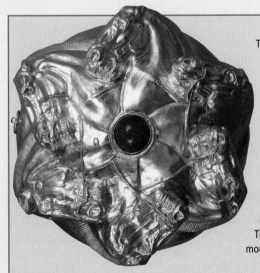

The Scythians owe their name to classical Greek historians, who used the term to describe horse-riding nomads living north of the Black Sea. Unbeknown to the Greeks, similar nomadic peoples could be found all the way across the steppes of Central Asia as far as eastern Siberia. As this relief molded on the base of a gold cup suggests, horses were central to their way of life: The Scythians traded them, rode them to move their herds of cattle between winter and summer pastures, and fought on them as mounted warriors. They buried dead leaders under massive earth mounds that have yielded many treasures.

WESTERN ASIA

👑 **c.600** In the South Pacific Polynesian voyagers from Fiji and Tonga sail east to settle the Cook and Society Islands.

EAST ASIA & OCEANIA

700–600 B.C.

THE ETRUSCANS IN ITALY

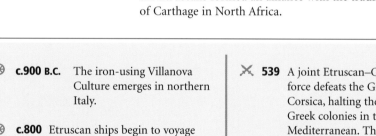

ANCIENT INHABITANTS OF A REGION *of central Italy known as Etruria, the Etruscans are one of history's mystery peoples. Although they were able to write, scholars today can decipher little of their script. Their literature, which was extensive, is lost except for a few fragments, and what we know of Etruscan history has come down to us through the unflattering comments of Greek and Roman writers.*

▲ The Etruscans grew rich by exploiting the mineral wealth of their land, which contained the only major sources of copper and iron in the central Mediterranean region. Their craftsmen used the metals to create magnificent artworks like this bronze statue of the Chimera—a monster with a lion's head and a snake tail.

Etruria, an area roughly equivalent to the modern Italian region of Tuscany, was rich in iron and copper ores. Its coastline possessed many natural harbors. Thus the Etruscans were skilled metalworkers and sailors. They grew rich by trading iron ingots, bronze, and other goods in their ships up and down the coast of Italy and across to southern France. By about 800 B.C., when Rome was still a hilltop cluster of huts, they had already begun to live in cities.

Etruscan traders faced competition from Phoenician and Greek traders in the western Mediterranean. In about 600 B.C. the Greeks founded a trading colony at Massilia (modern Marseille) in southern France. From this base they were able to seize control of the valuable trade route along the Rhône River into central Europe. To offset this loss, the Etruscans formed an alliance with the trading city of Carthage in North Africa.

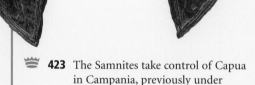

- ✳ **c.900 B.C.** The iron-using Villanova Culture emerges in northern Italy.

- ✳ **c.800** Etruscan ships begin to voyage along the west coast of Italy.

- ✳ **c.700** First use of Etruscan alphabetic script.

- 👑 **c.616** An Etruscan, Tarquin I, becomes king of Rome.

- 👑 **c.600** Twelve Etruscan cities come together to form the Etruscan League.

- 👑 **c.550** The Etruscans gain control of the Po Valley to the north of Etruria and begin to build cities there.

- ✕ **539** A joint Etruscan–Carthaginian force defeats the Greeks off Corsica, halting the spread of Greek colonies in the western Mediterranean. The Etruscans take control of Corsica.

- 👑 **c.525** The Etruscans establish a number of settlements in Campania (southern Italy).

- ✕ **525** The Etruscans unsuccessfully attack the Greek city of Cumae in southern Italy.

- 👑 **510** The Romans expel Tarquin II, the last Etruscan king of Rome.

- ✕ **504** The Etruscans suffer a major defeat in southern Italy at the Battle of Aricia.

- 👑 **423** The Samnites take control of Capua in Campania, previously under Etruscan rule.

- ✕ **405–396** The Romans capture the city of Veii in southern Etruria after a 10-year war.

- 👑 **c.400** The Gauls (Celts) cross the Alps to invade northern Italy and settle in the Po Valley. Etruscan power in the region begins to decline.

- ✕ **296–295** After a series of defeats by the Romans most of the Etruscan cities sign a truce with Rome.

- ✕ **285-280** Rome puts down a series of rebellions in the Etruscan cities.

The Etruscans were technologically advanced and built roads, bridges, and canals. They adopted the alphabet, vase painting, and temple building from the Greeks. During the 6th century B.C. the Etruscans expanded north and south out of their homeland of Etruria. According to Roman writers, 12 of the major Etruscan cities formed a loose political alliance, or "league" of states, at this time.

For a time Etruscan kings ruled the city of Rome. A group of Roman aristocrats overthrew the last Etruscan king of Rome in 510 B.C., an event that traditionally marked the foundation of the Roman Republic, and from that time on the Romans gradually replaced the Etruscans as the dominant power in Italy. The Etruscans finally disappeared from history early in the 3rd century B.C., swallowed up in the expanding political sphere of Rome.

The Romans took many cultural ideas from the Etruscans, such as augury—the belief that people can foretell the future by observing natural phenomena such as the flight of birds. They also inherited the Etruscans' knowledge of engineering and metalwork, and even some military tactics.

◀ There were Etruscan warriors, as this fearsome war helmet suggests. Yet the Etruscans are better known today for their artistic abilities, and in the long run they proved no match for the Romans as soldiers.

▶ The Etruscans' heartland lay in the region of Italy now known as Tuscany. They grew rich on sea trade, exporting metal ores from their mines, and used their wealth to spread their influence across much of northern Italy.

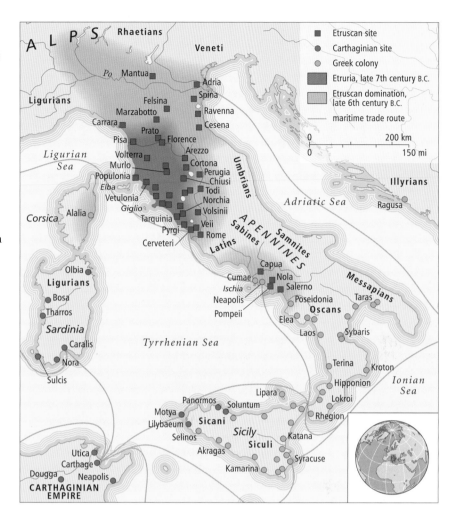

Cities of the Dead

The Etruscans buried their dead in extensive cemeteries that were laid out almost like cities. In southern Etruria they carved the tombs out of the soft tufa rock of the region and furnished them like houses. Such a tomb often contained a sculpted effigy of a deceased husband and wife reclining together on a couch, as if taking part in a banquet. Painted scenes of banquets attended by musicians and dancers decorated other tombs. Grave robbers have looted large numbers of the tombs, but archaeologists have excavated many that have survived the centuries intact. Their contents typically include enormous numbers of Greek vases, together with chariots and goods of gold, ivory, and amber, testifying to the wealth of the Etruscan aristocrats buried within them.

AMERICAS

c.600 The Paracas Culture flourishes on the Peruvian coast, producing spectacular colored textiles featuring a big-eyed figure known as the Oculate Being.

On a windswept peninsula on the coast of south-central Peru, a series of excavated burial sites have revealed the existence of an extraordinary early culture. Mummified by the dry desert heat, the Paracas corpses were laid to rest in richly decorated capes and blankets thought to have been specially woven by a local cottage industry.

EUROPE

c.594 Solon becomes sole archon (governor) of Athens. His laws lay the foundations of Athenian democracy.

585 The Greek philosopher Thales successfully predicts an eclipse of the sun.

578 Death of Tarquin I (Tarquinius Priscus), the first Etruscan ruler of Rome.

561 Peisistratus makes himself tyrant of Athens, dominating the city-state's politics for the next 34 years.

c.540 The Peloponnesian League unites most of the city-states of the Peloponnese, Greece's southern peninsula, under the leadership of Sparta.

539 The first known Greek tragedy is performed at Athens.

AFRICA

c.600 Carthaginians establish a colony at Marseille on the coast of southern France.

c.600 Iron- and bronzeworking develop in West Africa.

c.600 Phoenicians complete their circumnavigation of Africa.

591 Meroë becomes the capital of Nubia after Psammetichus II of Egypt sacks the former capital, Napata.

525 A Persian invasion force under Cambyses defeats Psammetichus III of Egypt at the Battle of Pelusium. For the next 121 years Egypt falls under Persian rule.

WESTERN ASIA

598 Judah rebels against Babylonian overlordship.

597 Nebuchadrezzar II conquers Jerusalem, but withdraws to quell a revolt at home.

597 Zedekiah is put on the throne of Judah by Nebuchadrezzar. He conspires with Egypt against the Babylonians.

c.590 The Zoroastrian religion spreads across Persia.

586 After a lengthy siege, Jerusalem falls to Nebuchadrezzar, who lays the city waste and takes many captives to Babylon.

585 Astyages succeeds his father Cyaxares as ruler of the short-lived empire of the Medes.

573 The Phoenician port of Tyre falls to Nebuchadrezzar's forces after a 13-year siege.

562 The death of Nebuchadrezzar marks the end of the great days of the Neo-Babylonian Empire.

560 Croesus becomes king of Lydia, a legendarily rich kingdom in Asia Minor (today's Turkey).

SOUTH & CENTRAL ASIA

599 Possible date of the birth of Mahavira ("Great Hero"), the founder of the Jain religion, which renounces the destruction of any living thing.

563 Possible date for the birth of Siddhartha Gautama, the Buddha, in India.

EAST ASIA & OCEANIA

c.600 The *Book of Songs*, the first anthology of Chinese poetry, is compiled.

551 Birth of Kongfuzi, known in the West as Confucius.

Confucius (Kongfuzi).

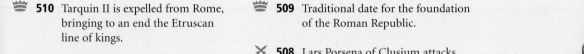
AMERICAS

☀ **c.600** The Middle Formative ceremonial centers of the Mayan region expand as populations in Central America continue to grow. New centers emerge at Cobá and Copán.

☀ **c.550** The Olmecs build a ceremonial center at Tres Zapotes in the Gulf Coast region.

☀ **c.500** Zapotecs establish a ceremonial center at Monte Albán in southern Mexico that flourishes for more than a thousand years.

⊕ **c.500** Corn-growing farmers settle the valleys around San Agustín in southern Colombia, which in time will become that country's most spectacular archaeological region.

EUROPE

🏛 **510** Tarquin II is expelled from Rome, bringing to an end the Etruscan line of kings.

🏛 **510** Cleisthenes overthrows Peisistratus's heirs, replacing tyranny with democracy in Athens.

🏛 **509** Traditional date for the foundation of the Roman Republic.

✕ **508** Lars Porsena of Clusium attacks Rome in an unsuccesful attempt to restore Etruscan rule.

Bronze cast of the type of mask worn by Greek tragic actors, c.500 B.C.

AFRICA

From humble beginnings, the Persian Cyrus built one of the ancient world's great empires. First conquering his overlords the Medes, he went on to defeat the Babylonians and Lydians. Under his successors Persia ruled a realm stretching from Egypt to the borders of India. Rich tribute like this Lydian bracelet flowed in to fill the imperial coffers.

⊕ **c.525** Camels are introduced into North Africa from Persia.

🏛 **c.500** The Bantu-speaking peoples begin to expand from their West African homeland.

WESTERN ASIA

🏛 **558** Cyrus becomes ruler of Persia.

✕ **550** Cyrus defeats his overlord, the Mede Astyages, launching Persia on the road to empire.

✕ **547** Cyrus defeats Croesus, sacking his capital of Sardis and bringing all of Asia Minor under Persian control.

✕ **539** Babylon falls to Cyrus, bringing Mesopotamia under Persian rule. Jewish exiles are permitted to return to Judah.

🏛 **530** Death of Cyrus the Great. He is succeeded by his son Cambyses, who conquers Egypt.

✕ **521** On Cambyses' death Darius comes to the Persian throne, putting down a number of revolts led by rival candidates.

☀ **c.515** The Temple in Jerusalem is rebuilt at the urging of the prophet Haggai.

📖 **c.500** The palace of Persepolis is built in Persia.

SOUTH & CENTRAL ASIA

🏛 **540** King Bimbisara rises to power in the Ganges kingdom of Magadha.

☀ **524** Gautama has the vision on which the Buddhist religion will be founded.

🏛 **521 on** Darius extends the borders of the Persian Empire beyond the Indus into northern India, defeating disunited Aryan forces.

EAST ASIA & OCEANIA

📖 **530** Confucius marries and enters the service of the duke of Lu.

🏛 **501** Confucius is made governor of the city of Chungtu.

600–500 B.C.

CONFUCIUS'S CHINA

CHINA PRODUCED THE FIRST *great East Asian civilization, boasting major philosophers and poets at a time when much of the rest of the world was still illiterate. In the works of later historians myth and reality blended in tales of legendary early dynasties peopled by hero-kings who were often credited with superhuman powers. Recent archaeological finds have shown that powerful, wealthy kings did indeed rule sizable kingdoms from ancient times.*

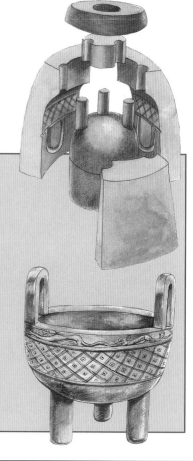

According to legend, China's civilization dates back to Huang Di, the Yellow Emperor, who ruled in about 2700 B.C. and invented boats, bows and arrows, and writing. In fact, the first dynasty (line of kings) that can be confirmed is the Shang, said to have come to power in 1766 B.C. The Shang were Bronze Age kings, sweeping into battle in metal chariots and practicing human sacrifice on a large scale. More positively, their era saw the birth of writing in China and the development of an accurate calendar.

In about 1027 B.C. the last Shang king was overthrown by Wu, king of Zhou in central China. The Zhou Dynasty that Wu founded was the longest lasting in Chinese history, surviving for 800 years. The Zhou claimed they had been granted a "Mandate of Heaven," giving the king absolute authority to rule as long as he took care of the welfare of his subjects.

Under the Zhou kings Chinese society developed on feudal lines into a pyramid with the king and

Bronze making in China

China's Bronze Age began sometime in the 3rd millennium B.C., when craftsmen learned to combine copper with tin or other metals to create bronze. By Shang Dynasty times bronze-working was well established. Early bronze vessels featured birds, dragons, and monster masks, but by the late 10th century B.C. the elements of the traditional *taotie* (an imaginary creature with horns, staring eyes, and a fearsome jaw) were incorporated into more abstract designs. Artifacts produced under the Zhou included weapons and spade-shaped coins, as well as sacrificial food vessels (*right*) to honor dead ancestors. The light vessels favored in the Shang period became more highly decorated and heavy bottomed.

---

c.1766 B.C. The Shang Dynasty is founded by King Tang.

c.1027 King Wu of Zhou overthrows the last Shang king and founds the Zhou Dynasty.

c.1000 Skilled bronze casting proliferates, with the *taotie* animal mask a favorite motif.

c.950 Death of King Mu, remembered in later legends as a world traveler.

c.800 Rapid urban expansion begins.

c.800 Wet rice cultivation and bronze technology are exported to Korea from China.

771 Barbarians and alienated Chinese nobility attack the Zhou capital and kill King Yu.

770 The Zhou capital moves from Hao to Luoyang, marking the start of the Eastern Zhou Dynasty; thereafter the power of the Zhou rulers declines as rival states battle for supremacy.

722–481 The *Spring and Autumn Annals* chronicle the history of the state of Lu, retrospectively giving their name to the period.

685 Huan of Qi assumes the role of hegemon, building up the economic power of the Qi state with the help of his minister Guan Zhong.

c.600 Ironworking begins to develop.

c.600 *Shi-jing* (The Book of Songs), a collection of 305 poems, reaches its final form.

c.600 The philosopher Lao-Tzu inspires Taoism, which urges disciples to connect to the *tao*, or "way," of nature.

551 The philosopher Confucius is born in the state of Lu.

c.550 After a period of prolonged interstate warfare the dual hegemony of the states of Jin and Chu ensures an uneasy peace for some years.

c.550 Cast iron is manufactured.

c.500 The *Analects*—a collection of Confucius's sayings as recorded by his disciples—is assembled.

c.500 Bronze coins are introduced.

◀ The Chinese were the only people to use the "piece-mold" system of casting for creating large vessels. In this method clay was pressed against a roughly patterned model to produce a mold. When dry, the mold was cut away in several pieces from the model, and more intricate designs were then carved into the clay. The pieces were reassembled upside down in a frame, and molten bronze was poured in. Finally, the mold was removed to reveal the finished bronze object.

▶ This elaborate jug with a stylized tiger's head for a lid shows just how skilled China's bronzeworkers had become by the late Shang period, in about 1200 B.C.

nobles at the top and millions of peasants at the bottom. Later historians saw its early years as a golden age of peace and stability. Things changed for the worse after a nobles' revolt in 771, when the ruling king was killed; the capital was then moved from Hao to Luoyang, 200 miles (350 km) to the east. The so-called Eastern Zhou kings who ruled thereafter reigned less securely than their Western predecessors. Having tasted power, the nobility proved unwilling to give it up, and central authority was weakened. China increasingly split into a number of states, each controlled by a dominant ruler, or "hegemon," owing only nominal loyalty to the Zhou king.

The first centuries of the Eastern Zhou era are known as the "Spring and Autumn" Period (722–481 B.C.), from the *Spring and Autumn Annals*, a chronicle detailing events in Lu, one of the empire's states. This was a time when the power of the states, each one controlled by a different noble family, was on the rise at the expense of the central power. Even so, the period saw much artistic and technological innovation and creativity. Bronze making reached new heights, ironworking developed, and the earliest Chinese poetry was composed. In addition, religious and philosophical thinkers came to the fore as people sought to find order in troubled times. The most influential of them, Confucius (551–479 B.C.), spent

his life traveling from court to court, teaching and advising. The *Analects*, compiled by his disciples, record his ideas: He emphasized humanity, respect for authority, and responsibility to others.

After Confucius's death the emperor's power was further eclipsed as the nation moved into a time of civil strife known as the Warring States Period (481–221). Through this dark era Confucianism—the ethical system based on the philosopher's thoughts—served as a beacon, and it remained a blueprint for social behavior in China until modern times.

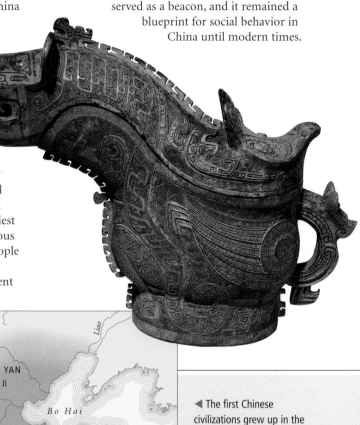

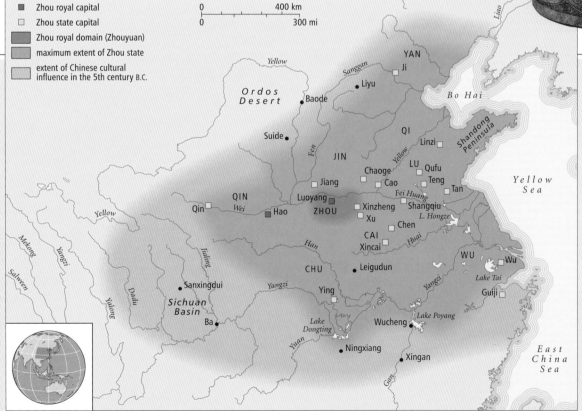

Zhou royal capital
Zhou state capital
Zhou royal domain (Zhouyuan)
maximum extent of Zhou state
extent of Chinese cultural influence in the 5th century B.C.

◀ The first Chinese civilizations grew up in the north of today's China, where the long-lasting Zhou Dynasty had its power base on the middle and lower reaches of the Huang (Yellow) River. Its first capital lay at Hao, on a western tributary of the river. But in time it proved too remote, and the capital was moved east to Luoyang in 770 B.C. Even so, the kings who ruled there could not prevent provincial nobles from developing power bases of their own in the various state capitals.

FACTS AT A GLANCE

Abraham
The founding father of the Jewish people, traditionally believed to have been born in the Mesopotamian city of Ur in about 1850 B.C. Abraham is also revered by Christians and by Muslims, who regard him as the ancestor of the Arabs through his son Ishmael.

Achaemenid Dynasty
The ruling dynasty of Persia from c.700 to 330 B.C. Under the Achaemenids Persia became the center of a huge empire stretching from India in the east to Libya in the west.

Adena Culture
A group of North American hunter-gatherer communities that settled in the Ohio River valley from c.1000 B.C. The culture was at its peak from c.700 to 100 B.C.; finds from sites include copper jewelry and decorated human skulls.

Aeolia
Ancient name for the coastal region of northwest Asia Minor, including the island of Lesbos, which was settled by Hellenic (Greek) peoples from c.850 B.C.

Ahab
King of Israel (c.873–852 B.C.), whose Phoenician wife Jezebel worshiped the god Baal. Ahab allied his forces with those of the king of Damascus to halt an Assyrian invasion at the Battle of Karkar (c.854 B.C.).

Ahmose
Pharaoh of Egypt from c.1550 to 1525 B.C. whose reign inaugurated the New Kingdom Period. He completed the task, begun by his father Kamose, of driving the Hyksos rulers out of Lower Egypt and so reuniting the two halves of the kingdom.

Akhenaten
Literally "Spirit of the Aten"; the name adopted by the Egyptian New Kingdom Pharaoh Amenhotep IV (c.1353–1336 B.C.) in c.1350 B.C. in line with his policy of replacing the worship of Egypt's many gods with the cult of a single deity, the *aten*, or sun's disk.

Akhetaten
The city built in around 1348 B.C. by Akhenaten to replace Thebes as the capital of New Kingdom Egypt. Akhetaten was devoted to the cult of the *aten*, or sun's disk, whereas Thebes was the stronghold of the high priests of the old religion. Akhetaten was abandoned not long after Akhenaten's death, when the old faith was restored. Today the site is known as Tell el-Amarna.

Akkadians
A people speaking a Semitic language who inhabited a region to the north of Sumer in the mid-3rd millennium B.C. They rose to prominence from c.2350 B.C. under a charismatic ruler, Sargon the Great, who made their capital city, Akkad, the center of a significant (if short-lived) empire.

Alaca Höyük
A royal burial site of the early Bronze Age in central Turkey. In each small, roofed tomb the body was placed centrally, knees drawn up to the stomach, and accompanied by rich gifts in bronze and precious metals.

Al Mina
Trading post established by the Greek city-state of Euboea around 800 B.C. at the mouth of the Orontes River in what is now eastern Turkey. Al Mina provided contacts not only with local traders but also with merchants from central and eastern Anatolia and Mesopotamia.

Amenhotep I
Also known as Amenophis I; Egyptian pharaoh of Egypt's 18th Dynasty, reigning c.1525–1504 B.C. The second pharaoh of the New Kingdom, Amenhotep continued the expansionist policies of his father Ahmose, pushing south into Nubia and inaugurating a new period of monument building.

Arameans
A Semitic people who moved east from the Syrian desert to occupy the northern reaches of the Euphrates River. By the 11th century B.C. they were encroaching on Assyrian territory in southern Anatolia and northern Arabia. The Arameans were conquered by the Assyrians in the 9th century B.C., but their Aramaic language survived to become the common tongue of West Asia for the next thousand years.

Archaic Period (Egypt)
The period from c.3100 to 2575 B.C. when Egypt's scattered chiefdoms were brought under the rule of a unified state but the full pharaonic traditions of the Old Kingdom had yet to emerge.

Archaic Period (Greece)
Starting around 750 B.C., the time in which Greek civilization began to emerge from the relative economic, political, and cultural stagnation of the "Dark Age."

Ark of the Covenant
In Jewish tradition the container that God ordered Moses to build in order to house the stones inscribed with the Ten Commandments; its precise specifications are given in Exodus 25:1–22.

Aryans
Warlike peoples believed to have originated on the Eurasian steppes (grassland) who swept across the Persian plateau and into northern India sometime after 2000 B.C. Other Aryan groups are thought to have headed for China and Europe. The Aryan language is believed to have been the ancestor of all the various Indo-European tongues, including Sanskrit.

Assurnarsipal II
Assyrian king who reigned from around 883 to 858 B.C. Renowned for his cruelty, he used barbaric punishments to terrorize enemy peoples into submission. Under his rule the Assyrian empire expanded to reach the Mediterranean for the first time in 200 years.

Assyrians
A warlike people from northern Mesopotamia who dominated West Asia from the 14th to the late 7th centuries B.C. At its peak in the 8th century the Assyrian empire stretched over most of the lands of the Fertile Crescent.

astrologer
A person who studies the relative position of the planets and stars in the belief that they influence events on Earth. The idea that the movements of the heavenly bodies affect human lives was first developed by the Babylonians.

Avebury
A village in the English county of Wiltshire that is the site of Europe's largest stone circle, with a maximum diameter of 1,350 feet (412 m). The monument was constructed c.2300–1800 B.C. as a ritual center.

Babylon
The main city of ancient Mesopotamia, located on the Euphrates River and first settled c. 3000 B.C. It was the capital of two successive empires separated by almost 1,000 years: the Old Babylonian Empire (c.1750–1595 B.C.) and the Neo-Babylonian Empire (c.600–539 B.C.).

Ban Kao Culture
Named after a site in southern Thailand, this distinctive Neolithic culture created remarkably accomplished pottery, stone tools, and jewelry. Its influence extended well down the Malay Peninsula.

Beaker People
People thought to have been of Iberian origin who spread out over Europe in the 3rd millennium B.C. Their sites are identified by distinctive earthenware beakers, which were placed in burial chambers to hold a drink for the dead on their last journey.

Brahmanas
Written at the start of the 8th century B.C. in India, these texts are interpretive commentaries on the Vedas, explaining the content of the hymns and the rituals they prescribe.

Brahmins
The supreme social rank, or "caste," of Aryan society in northern India, a ruling elite of priests. Beneath them were the *kshatriya* (warriors), the *vaishya* (traders and farmers), and the mass of *shudra* (non-Aryan servants).

Bronze Age
A period of technological development between the Stone Age and the Iron Age during which bronze was commonly used to make weapons and tools. It began in West Asia in the 4th millennium B.C.

Canaan
A region of western Asia between the Mediterranean and Dead Seas. The home of various Canaanite city-states in the 2nd millennium B.C., it was conquered c.1200 B.C. by the Israelites, who regarded it as the land promised by God to their founding father Abraham.

Carthage
The Phoenicians' most famous colony, established c.814 B.C. on the coast of North Africa near present-day Tunis. It became an important commercial center, controlling a trading empire stretching to southern Spain and the western Mediterranean islands. By the time it was destroyed by the Romans in 146 B.C., its population had grown to more than half a million.

Celts
People speaking related Celtic languages who spread out from Central Europe c.1000 B.C. to inhabit parts of France, Germany, Iberia (Spain and Portugal), and the British Isles. Celtic languages survive in Brittany, Ireland, Wales, and Scotland.

Chaldeans
A Semitic people inhabiting a region of ancient Babylonia. The Chaldeans became dominant in the region, establishing a Babylonian dynasty from 626 to 539 B.C.

Chavín Culture
The first great culture of ancient Peru, named for the Andean town of Chavín de Huantar where its first artifacts were excavated in 1919. Chavín-style temple complexes featured flat-topped pyramids, central plazas, and huge stone relief carvings. The culture flourished for almost 1,000 years, from c.1200 to 300 B.C.

Chinchorro Culture
A culture based in a few fishing villages on what is now the Peru–Chile border that practiced mummification of the dead as early as c.5000 B.C., about 2,500 years before the Egyptians started mummifying bodies.

Chorreran Culture
A culture based in Ecuador from 1200 to 300 B.C., marked by a distinctive style of pottery.

Confucius
Celebrated Chinese administrator and philosopher (551–479 B.C.), known in China as Kongfuzi. His teachings, emphasizing learning, respect, and good conduct, became a state religion in China.

cuneiform
A form of writing using wedge-shaped marks (*cuneus* being Latin for "wedge") developed by the Sumerians about 3000 B.C. Cuneiform characters were impressed in wet clay or wax with the pointed end of a reed.

Cyaxares
The best-known king of the Medes, Cyaxares conquered the Assyrians in around 612 B.C., creating a short-lived Medean Empire. The Medes were themselves defeated by the Persians soon after, however, and became merged in the Persian Empire.

Cyclades
A group of islands in the Aegean Sea between Greece and Turkey, the Cyclades are famous for abstract sculpted figures crafted during the 3rd millennium B.C. They were produced from a local marble that split easily, which meant that the sculptors concentrated on producing essential forms rather than details.

Cyrus the Great
Ruler of Persia from 558 to 530 B.C. and the creator of the mighty Persian Empire. Having freed Persia from subjection to the Medes in 550 B.C., Cyrus went on to defeat Lydia in 547 and to conquer Babylon in 539, winning control of a realm stretching from the Mediterranean to the borders of India.

David
First king of Israel's Judean dynasty, reigning c.1006–965 B.C. David became king of Judah on the death of Saul and was later chosen to be ruler of a united Israel. David made Jerusalem the kingdom's capital, building a palace (the "city of David") on its highest hill, Zion.

diaspora
A dispersion or spreading; specifically the dispersal of Jews around the world after the Babylonian and Roman conquests of Palestine.

Djoser
A pharaoh of Egypt's 3rd Dynasty who ruled c.2650 B.C. Djoser is most famous for his spectacular "Step Pyramid," designed as his final resting place by his chief associate, Imhotep.

dolmen
A prehistoric burial chamber consisting of a stone slab laid on two or more upright stones. Dolmens are most numerous in northwest Europe but are also found in North Africa and as far east as Japan.

domestication
The process of bringing wild plants and animals under human control. At first humans domesticated certain plants and animals to secure a reliable food source. Later they bred animals such as the horse and ass as beasts of burden.

Dorians
Nomadic herdsmen and raiders believed to have wandered westward into Greece from Asia Minor (modern Turkey) in the 11th Century B.C. The Dorians spread death and destruction in their path, but also brought with them knowledge of ironworking.

Dorset Culture
Culture that spread across the American Arctic in the 8th century B.C., based around the hunting of walruses, seals, and other sea mammals. With its exquisite little figures, frequently human, and its razor-sharp harpoon heads and blades, it represented a clear artistic and technological advance on the "small tools" tradition it replaced.

Draco
A Greek lawgiver who in 621 B.C. prepared the first written laws for Athens. Draco's laws made even minor crimes punishable by death; the term "draconian" is still used today to describe harsh laws or severe punishment.

dynasty
A succession of rulers from the same family, their power handed down from father to son (or, in some cases, daughter). Between 2950 and 343 B.C. 30 different dynasties ruled in Egypt.

Elamites
People of a kingdom based in western Iran that conquered the Sumerian city of Ur in c.1950 B.C. and later exerted influence on the rulers of Babylon and Assyria.

Etruria
The land of the Etruscans between the Tiber and Arno rivers in Italy.

Etruscan League
A loose economic and religious league formed among 12 Etruscan city-states in the 6th century B.C. It may have been modeled on similar confederations in Greece.

Etruscans
Inhabitants of Etruria, the dominant civilization in Italy between 800 and 300 B.C. The Etruscan city-states were eventually conquered by the Romans, who adopted many features of Etruscan civilization.

Exodus
The escape of the Jews led by Moses from exile in pharaonic Egypt, as described in the biblical Book of Exodus. Egyptian sources make no reference to the event, which may have taken place in the reign of the pharaoh Merneptah (c.1224–1214 B.C.).

Fertile Crescent
A semicircle of formerly fertile land stretching across West Asia from Israel through what is now Lebanon and Syria and then down the length of Mesopotamia to the Persian Gulf. Settled agriculture and the world's earliest civilizations developed in the region.

Gauls
Celtic-speaking peoples who inhabited France and Belgium in Roman times. Although divided into different tribes, the Gauls shared a common religion controlled by priests, called druids, who came from noble families.

Gilgamesh
Sumerian ruler of Uruk who may have reigned around 2750 B.C. His life and adventures were later recorded in fictionalized form in the *Epic of Gilgamesh*, where he is portrayed as a brave but tragic character striving for fame and immortality.

Great Pyramid
The largest Egyptian pyramid, with a height of 480 feet (146 m) and smooth sides angled at 52° to the horizontal. Built at Giza as the tomb of King Khufu in around 2550 B.C., it is the only one of the Seven Wonders of the Ancient World to have survived to the present day.

Hallstatt Culture
An Iron Age culture of the ancient Celts, named after the town in Austria where its remains were first identified in the mid-19th century near ancient salt mines. Its influence was strongest in the lands around the headwaters of the Danube River.

Hammurabi I
As ruler of Babylon from c.1792 to 1750 B.C., Hammurabi turned an insignificant state into a mighty empire. He introduced a famous law code that covered everything from class privilege and property rights to questions of personal morality.

Harappa
A large city and commercial center of the Indus Civilization in the Punjab region of present-day Pakistan. Like Mohenjo-Daro, it was laid out on a grid pattern with standardized, brick-built housing.

Hatshepsut
The most famous of Egypt's few female pharaohs, reigning from c.1473 to 1458 B.C. Coming to power as regent for her infant son Thutmose III, Hatshepsut took power in her own name and proved an effective ruler; in particular, she did much to develop Egypt's international trade.

Hattusas
The Hittite capital, located in the mountains of central Anatolia, near the modern village of Boghazköy. Even in ruins it remains impressive, proclaiming the power—and the unabashed militarism—of its founders.

Hebrew
An Israelite, or the descendant of one of a group of northern Semitic peoples including the Israelites; also the language of the ancient Hebrews and any of various later forms of this language.

hegemon
The name given in ancient Greece to a leader who dominated or had authority over other rulers within a region; the most powerful figure within a confederation.

Hesiod
Greek poet who was the author, around 700 B.C., of the first known works of written Greek literature. In addition to his *Theogony*, detailing the lives of the Greek gods, he also wrote a book on agriculture, *Works and Days*.

hieroglyphics
A system of writing used by the ancient Egyptians and based at first on the pictorial representation of things; soon, however, a phonetic (sound-based) element evolved to supplement these images, giving it greater flexibility.

Hittites
A warlike people of uncertain origin who established a state in central Anatolia in the mid-16th century B.C. and went on to extend their dominion through much of the Middle East. Hittite military success owed much to their skilled use of three-man war chariots. They remained a force in the region for almost 500 years, only to be wiped off the map by unknown assailants around the year 1200 B.C.

Homer
By tradition, the blind author of two great Greek epic poems, the *Iliad* and the *Odyssey*, believed to have been composed in the 8th century B.C. In fact both works may well contain much older passages that had been passed down orally (by word of mouth) by generations of bards.

hominids
Extinct ancestors of humans that evolved from African apes between 12 and 2.5 million years ago. Several different hominid species have been identified. Their main humanlike features were two-legged walking, increased brain size, and the use of tools.

Homo erectus
"Upright man," a species of early human that lived in Africa, Asia, and Europe between about 1.8 and 0.5 million years ago. *Homo erectus* used axes and were the first humans to make and control fire.

Homo sapiens
"Wise man," the species name given to modern humans, who first emerged in Africa about 160,000 years ago.

Hoshea
The last ruler of the kingdom of Israel (c.730–721 B.C.), who rebelled against Assyrian rule. In response the Assyrians captured Samaria, marking the end of the northern kingdom (although the southern Israelite kingdom of Judah survived).

Huang Di
The mythical "Yellow Emperor" of ancient Chinese legend, supposed to have founded Chinese civilization in 2698 B.C.

hunter-gatherers
People who live off the land in small nomadic groups, feeding themselves by hunting game and gathering nuts, berries, seeds, and other plant foods. All humans lived as hunter-gatherers in the centuries before the development of agriculture; a few small hunter-gatherer groups still survive to this day.

Hyksos
Middle Eastern immigrants to Egypt who built a power base in the Nile Delta around their capital at Avaris. Eventually (in c.1640 B.C.) they gained control of Lower Egypt, while also forcing the Egyptian rulers of Upper Egypt to pay them tribute. The time of their ascendancy is known as the Second Intermediate Period.

ice age
Any of several periods of severe global cooling, the last of which ended about 10,000 years ago. During the coldest phases of the ice age ice sheets spread as far south as New England.

Iliad
Homer's stirring account of the siege of Troy, the heroes who fought on both sides, and the gods and goddesses who interfered in their affairs.

Indus Valley Civilization
The first great Indian civilization, which covered about 500,000 square miles (1.3 million sq km) of territory along and around the Indus Valley.

Ionians
Migrants from mainland Greece who colonized the southern Aegean coast of Asia Minor (today's Turkey) and its offshore islands, many passing through the growing port of Athens as they fled the advance of overland invaders from the north.

irrigation
Artificial watering of dry agricultural areas by means of dams and channels.

Israelite
Member of an ethnic group claiming descent from Jacob, a Hebrew; also, in a more limited sense, a citizen of the northern kingdom of Israel (c.925–721 B.C.).

Jebusites
A people of unknown origin (possibly refugees from the crumbling Hittite Empire) who occupied the citadel of Zion before King David and his Jews seized it for their capital around 1000 B.C.

Jehu
King of Israel from c.842 to 815 B.C. who, encouraged by Israel's prophets, halted the cult of Baal in his country by killing Jezebel, the widow of his predecessor King Ahab, along with the rest of Ahab's family and the priests of Baal. The violence weakened Israel, and Jehu ended up having to pay tribute to Assyria.

Jimmu
Mythical first emperor of Japan, believed to be a direct descendant of the Sun Goddess.

Joshua
In the Bible the man who, after Moses's death, led the Israelites in the conquest of Canaan and the creation of a homeland.

Judah
A son of the Biblical patriarch Jacob; also the name of the tribal territory of his descendants and, after the division of the Hebrew kingdom, the name of the southern Israelite kingdom, whose capital was at Jerusalem.

Kadesh, Battle of
A hard-fought and mutually draining encounter between Ramses II's Egyptian forces and Muwatallis's Hittites in c.1285 B.C. Both sides claimed victory, but signed a nonaggression pact in the battle's aftermath.

Kashta
A king of Nubia in the 8th century B.C., Kashta took much of southern Egypt under Kushite (Nubian) rule—a hold that was only strengthened under his son Piye.

Khephren
Also known as Khafra or Chephren; the fourth pharaoh of Egypt's 4th Dynasty, ruling in the latter part of the 26th century B.C. Khephren is today remembered as the builder of the second largest of the three pyramids at Giza and also of the Sphinx, which guards it. This gigantic, lion-bodied, human-headed statue would eventually be worshiped as a deity.

Khufu
Also known as Cheops; the second pharaoh of Egypt's 4th Dynasty, ruling for over 20 years in the first half of the 26th century B.C. The Great Pyramid was constructed to house his body after death; the largest of the three pyramids at Giza, it was also the first to be built.

Knossos
The majestic palace complex on the coast of Crete around which the Minoan culture centered. The palace's mazelike basement inspired the legend of the Labyrinth and its attendant Minotaur (half-man and half-bull), but was probably used for storing produce.

Kush
An independent African kingdom on the Nile River that emerged from the Egyptian province of Nubia in the 10th century B.C. In the 8th century B.C. under King Kashta it extended its rule into Egypt, providing that country with its 25th dynasty of pharaohs. The Kushites were strongly influenced by Egyptian customs, worshiping Egyptian gods and burying their kings in stone pyramids.

La Galgada
A temple mound built c.2300 B.C. by communal labor in northern Peru. The temple contained small rooms with central fireplaces where offerings to the gods were burned.

Lagash
A Sumerian city-state that emerged as a major power in southern Mesopotamia around 2500 B.C. Much of our knowledge of Sumerian society, religion, and politics comes from thousands of inscribed clay tablets found at Lagash.

Lao-tzu
Chinese philosopher whose teachings are supposed to have inspired Taoism. The philosophy's chief work, the *Tao-te-Ching* or Way of Power, was written down about 300 years after Lao-tzu's death.

Lapita Culture
A Stone Age Oceanian culture characterized above all by its richly decorative pottery, made from c.1300 B.C. on. The Lapita people were great ocean voyagers, and anthropologists have used finds of Lapita pottery to track the colonization of the islands of eastern Melanesia and Polynesia.

La Venta
Ceremonial center in the Tabasco region of Mexico that became the focus of the Olmec Culture after the destruction of San Lorenzo.

Longshan Culture
A Chinese culture based in large, fortified villages that spread out from the lower and middle Yellow River valley c.2500–1950 B.C. Famous for its refined black pottery, Longshan culture also produced the first known bronze artifacts in China.

Lothal
A major port of the Indus Civilization, located in what is now the Indian state of Gujarat. Lothal was an important trade link between India and Mesopotamia.

Lucy
The name given to the 3.5 million-year-old fossil remains of a female hominid discovered in 1974 in Ethiopia. The structure of Lucy's skeleton, assigned to the species *Australopithecus afarensis*, indicated that she could walk upright.

lugal
A Sumerian word, literally meaning "great man," that came to mean "king." We know the names of some Sumerian *lugals* from a surviving king list, a semifactual record of Sumerian rulers from c.3000 to 1800 B.C.

lur
A prehistoric Scandinavian wind instrument, possibly used for ceremonial purposes and also in battle to rally troops and frighten the enemy.

Lydia

A wealthy kingdom in western Asia Minor (Turkey) that flourished in the 7th and 6th centuries B.C. The first state to use coined money, Lydia was conquered by the Persians in 547 B.C.

Magadha

A Hindu state that dominated the Ganges Delta region of eastern India in the 6th century B.C.

Mahabharata

Indian epic poem describing the dynastic power struggles of a line of Aryan rulers in northern India, possibly in the 10th century B.C. The work of many different hands, it was probably written down around 300 B.C.–100 A.D., although it contains material passed down orally (by word of mouth) from much earlier times.

Maya

A native people of southeastern Mexico and Central America. Mayan civilization reached its height around 300–900 A.D. but its roots can be traced back to as early as 1500 B.C.

Medes

An Indo-European people who allied with Babylon to conquer Assyria in 612 B.C., bringing to an end the days of Assyrian greatness. The Medes went on to establish a short-lived empire but were themselves subjugated by Persia in 550 B.C.

Megiddo

City in what is now northern Israel that was taken after a seven-month siege by Pharaoh Thutmose III in c.1456 B.C. The Egyptian victory destroyed a coalition of Canaanite princes recognizing the overlordship of Mitanni and opened the way for the expansion of Egyptian power into Syria.

Memphis

The earliest capital of a united Egypt, founded by King Menes c.2950 B.C.

Mentuhotep II

The founding pharaoh of the Middle Kingdom who reunited Upper and Lower Egypt in c.2040 B.C. A strong, centralizing ruler, he restored order to an Egypt torn apart by the feuding of the First Intermediate Period.

Mesopotamia

An ancient Greek name meaning "between the rivers," applied to the fertile land between the Tigris and Euphrates rivers in southern Iraq. Here the Sumerians, Babylonians, and Assyrians established their civilizations.

Midas

A famously rich ruler of Phrygia in the 8th century B.C.; according to Greek legend, everything he touched turned to gold. He was killed by Cimmerian invaders from the Black Sea region.

Middle Kingdom

The second main period of Egyptian prosperity and power, lasting from c.2040 to 1640 B.C., when the pharaohs of the 11th–13th Dynasties restored unified rule to Egypt and further centralized government, while also extending the amount of cultivable land in the Nile Valley and expanding southward into Nubia.

Minoan Culture

The artistically dazzling culture that flourished on the eastern Mediterranean island of Crete in the 2nd and 3rd millennia B.C. The high point of Minoan culture was reached in the so-called "palace" era between c.2000 and 1450 B.C., when luxurious dwellings were built for the island's rulers at Knossos and other centers.

Minos

A legendary ruler of Crete who gave his name to the island's Minoan culture.

Mittani

A kingdom in northern Mesopotamia that grew in power through the mid-16th century B.C., first turning back an expansionist Egypt and then allying with the pharaohs against the Hittites. It then fell into decline, and by the end of the 14th century B.C. its lands had been divided between the Hittite and Assyrian empires.

Mohenjo-Daro

A large city of the Indus Valley Civilization on the Indus River in present-day Pakistan. Dating from around 2500 B.C., the city was laid out on a grid pattern, with main roads up to 30 feet (9 m) across and sidestreets up to 10 feet (3 m) wide.

mortuary cult

The worship of the dead—especially dead kings—as divine protectors of the living. In Egypt such devotion inspired the construction of the pyramids and the practice of mummification.

Mount Thera

A volcano on the island of Santorini in the southern Aegean whose eruption in the mid-15th century B.C. brought about the destruction of the cities of Minoan Crete.

Mycenae

A fortified city near the coast of the Pelepponesian Peninsula in southern Greece that became the center of a Bronze Age civilization that flourished c.1600–1250 B.C. Mycenaean Greeks conquered Minoan Crete and besieged Troy.

Nabopolassar

The founder in 626 B.C. of the Chaldean dynasty of Babylonian kings. Under his successor Nebuchadrezzar II Babylon became the center of the Neo-Babylonian Empire.

Naqada

One of the earliest towns to develop in ancient Egypt and the site where evidence of a prepharaonic society was first unearthed in the late 19th century. Its name is now often applied to the culture of Egypt's late predynastic period, in the 4th millennium B.C.

Neanderthals

A race of early humans whose remains were first identified in the Neander Valley, Germany. The Neanderthals lived in Europe and West Asia in the last ice age, from around 120,000 to 28,000 years ago. Their last traces have been found in the Iberian Peninsula; after that they either died out or, possibly, merged into the main *Homo sapiens* population.

Nebuchadrezzar II

Also (more familiarly but less correctly) known as Nebuchadnezzar. A Chaldean king of Babylon (604–562 B.C.), he presided over and expanded the Neo-Babylonian Empire, whose foundations had been laid by his father Nabopolassar's defeat of the Assyrians in 612. Nebuchadrezzar also rebuilt the city of Babylon, endowing it with the famous Hanging Gardens that were one of the Seven Wonders of the Ancient World. His forces captured Jerusalem in 597 and returned to destroy it in 586 B.C., carrying off many Israelites into Babylonian captivity.

Necho II

One of the greatest of the late Egyptian pharaohs, ruling from 610 to 595 B.C., Necho is remembered for his wars against Nebuchadrezzar's Babylonians and his attempt to link the Nile to the Red Sea by means of a canal. He also developed a powerful Egyptian navy.

Neolithic

Adjective referring to the New Stone Age, the final period of the Stone Age, starting c.10,000 years ago, in which hunter-gatherers learned to domesticate plant and animal species and started settling down to an agricultural way of life.

New Kingdom
The period from c.1550 to 1070 B.C. when Egypt was ruled by the pharaohs of the 18th to 20th dynasties. A time of prosperity, territorial expansion, and ambitious building projects, the New Kingdom period is widely regarded as the high point of ancient Egyptian civilization.

Nile Delta
The broad, marshy plain across which the Nile fans out in innumerable smaller channels as it reaches the Mediterranean Sea. The pharaohs ruled this area as part of Lower Egypt.

Nubia
A region of Africa directly beyond Egypt's southern border, centered on the Nile Valley and roughly corresponding with modern Sudan. Nubia's fate was always closely linked with that of Egypt: At times it was conquered and pillaged by the pharaohs' armies, at others it was seen either as an important trading partner or as a military threat. The kingdom of Kush, which rose to power in Nubia in the 10th century B.C., eventually provided Egypt with a dynasty of Nubian pharaohs.

Odyssey
Homer's famous epic poem describing the adventures that befell the Greek hero Odysseus on his long journey home from the Trojan War.

Old Kingdom
The first great age of Egyptian civilization, usually dated c.2575–2125 B.C. and taking in the reigns of the 4th to 8th dynasties of pharaohs; some authorities, however, also include the first three dynasties of Early Dynastic pharaohs within its scope, pushing its origins back to c.2950 B.C. The Old Kingdom was a time of political stability that laid the seeds for 3,000 years of ancient Egyptian culture; today it is particularly remembered as the Age of the Pyramids.

Olmecs
A people who flourished c.1250–200 B.C. in southern Mexico and parts of Guatemala, Honduras, and Costa Rica, and who were responsible for the first great culture of the Central American region. Olmec culture is famous particularly for its ceremonial centers and for its colossal stone heads.

Olympic Games
First held in 776 B.C., the ancient (like the modern) Olympic Games were held every four years, in their case at Olympia in the Peloponnese. The games brought together champion athletes from Greece's scattered city-states to compete in running, wrestling, and other athletic events.

papyrus
A type of paper made by the ancient Egyptians from the crushed stems of the papyrus reed.

Perdiccas I
The first king of Macedon, who, according to tradition, drove eastward from the Greek city of Argos to carve out a separate kingdom in northern Greece in the mid-7th century B.C.

Persians
A people of ancient Iran who established an empire in southwest Asia under Cyrus the Great, conquering first the Medes to their north then the Neo-Babylonian Empire to their east.

pharaoh
The title given to the rulers of ancient Egypt. Pharaohs were worshiped as gods and were responsible for maintaining *maat*—good order—on Earth.

Phoenicians
Seafaring traders from the coast of present-day Lebanon who set up trading colonies around the Mediterranean as early as 1000 B.C.

Phrygia
Ancient country of west-central Asia Minor that rose to prominence from c.1200 B.C., when settlers from eastern Europe moved in to occupy territories formerly belonging to the collapsed Hittite realm.

Phung Nyugen
A Neolithic culture that flourished from c.4,000 years ago in northern Vietnam; by 1500 B.C. it had evolved into the Dong Dau Bronze Age culture.

pictograph
A picture used in early writing to represent an object.

polis
The origin of the modern word "politics," it was the independent city-state that became characteristic of classical Greece. Although city-states sometimes fell under the control of tyrants, they also often acted as testing grounds for the concept of democracy; even though democratic rights were invariably limited, their citizens still seem to have felt involved and empowered.

Polynesians
Seafaring people who probably originated in Southeast Asia and the East Indies and whose progess was marked by the spread of the Lapita culture. Notable for their navigational skills and double-hulled dugout canoes, they settled Samoa and Tonga by c.1000 B.C.

Poverty Point Culture
A transitional phase between the Archaic (hunter-gatherer) and Formative (settled agricultural) stages of development among the native peoples of the American South. Taking its name from an archaeological site in Louisiana, where the earliest known earthworks in North America were found, its influence eventually extended to sites from Florida to Arkansas.

radiometric dating
A method of measuring the passage of time by means of the rate of decay of radioactive elements.

Ramses II
As pharaoh c.1290–1224 B.C., Ramses II, "the Great," ruled Egypt in a time of great prosperity and left many monuments, including the famous Abu Simbel temple. His early ambitions to expand the Egyptian empire northward into Syria came to an end in stalemate at the Battle of Kadesh. Thereafter he made peace with his Hittite enemies and devoted the rest of his long reign to efficient government and large-scale construction projects.

Ramses III
The last of the great New Kingdom pharaohs (c.1194–1163 B.C.), Ramses III saved Egypt from invasion by the Sea Peoples, but could not prevent the beginnings of a slide into instability that gathered momentum through his successors' reigns.

Rehoboam
Son of Solomon, reigning from 928 to 911 B.C., who so angered the northern Israelite tribes that they split from the southern kingdom of Judah to form the separate kingdom of Israel.

Rig-Veda
The world's oldest sacred text. A compilation of 1,028 Hindu hymns grouped into ten books, it started to take shape from c.1500 B.C. and was probably given its final shape c.900 B.C.

Romans
A tribe of shepherds living in the hills of west-central Italy before they founded the city of Rome in the 8th century B.C., the Romans would in time go on to conquer much of the known world.

San Lorenzo
A ceremonial center in southern Mexico where the beginnings of Olmec civilization are found. Perched on a clay platform 150 feet (45 m) high, symmetrical earth banks clustered around rectanguar courtyards that were decorated with colossal stone heads (probably portraits of Olmec leaders) and carved basalt slabs.

Sanskrit
The common language of culture in Aryan India and the ancestor of many modern Indian tongues; in its pure form it is studied by scholars of the classical Hindu texts.

Sappho
A Greek poetess who lived c.600 B.C. on the island of Lesbos. Her poems are personal and candid.

Sargon of Akkad
King of Akkad (a site somewhere on the Euphrates River in northern Mesopotamia that has not yet identified) who conquered the Sumerians c.2350 B.C. and founded the world's first empire, extending from the Persian Gulf to Syria and Iran.

Sargon II
As king of Assyria c.727–705 B.C., Sargon II continued the rebuilding of the empire undertaken by his father Tiglath-Pileser. He relied as much on agile diplomacy as on generalship to achieve his ends.

Saul
The first king (c.1020–1006 B.C.) elected by the Israelites. The Bible graphically describes his jealousy of his son-in-law David, who eventually succeeded him as ruler.

scribe
A man skilled in writing—a key figure in many ancient societies. Chronicles kept by scribes gave a state its historical self-image; their recordkeeping ensured its economic effectiveness.

Scythians
Nomadic tribespeople from Central Asia who were skilled horsemen and archers. Scythian leaders were buried in tombs with gold jewelry and horse sacrifices.

Sea Peoples
Raiders who caused disruption throughout the eastern Mediterranean region toward the end of the 2nd millennium B.C. They left no direct legacy, but their activities affected all the great West Asian civilizations of the age.

Second Intermediate Period
The period from c.1640 to 1550 B.C. in which a succession of Asiatic Hyksos rulers held power in Lower Egypt. Unified rule was eventually restored by Ahmose, the ruler of Upper Egypt, and the pharaohs of the ensuing New Kingdom.

Semitic
The language group of various southwest Asian peoples, including the Babylonians, Assyrians, and Hebrews. Semitic peoples founded the religions of Judaism, Christianity, and Islam.

Sennacherib
Sargon II's successor as Assyrian king (c.705–681 B.C.), Sennacherib built a majestic new capital at Nineveh. Thwarted in his attempts to capture Jerusalem, he retook a rebellious Babylon and sacked it in 689 B.C.

Senusret II
A pharaoh of the 12th Dynasty who reigned c.1897–1878 B.C. The irrigation improvements he made around the Fayyum oasis radically extended Egypt's productive agricultural area, with profound economic consequences for the state.

Shabako
Shabako reasserted Kushite (Nubian) authority over all Egypt and, by setting up his court at Thebes, effectively extended the rule of a dynasty (the 25th) of Nubian pharaohs over the whole country.

Shalmaneser III
King of Assyria from c.858 to 824 B.C. who spent much of his long reign battling for control of northern Syria.

Shang Dynasty
The earliest Chinese dynasty for which there is direct archaeological evidence. Traditionally dated from 1766 to 1027 B.C., it held sway over much of northern China. Its rulers were buried in deep pits accompanied by many human sacifices.

Shoshenq I
Also known as Sheshonk I and, in the Bible, as Shishak. Libyan pharaoh of Egypt (c.945–924 B.C.) who presided over a revival of Egyptian fortunes. He invaded Judah and Israel in 924 B.C., forcing the Israelites to pay tribute to Egypt.

Skara Brae
A prehistoric settlement on the Orkney Islands, Scotland. Occupied until about 2500 B.C., the settlement is well preserved because the houses were sunk into the ground and were built entirely of stone, including the furniture.

Sneferu
As pharaoh (c.2575–2551 B.C.) and founder of the 4th Dynasty, Sneferu placed pyramid building at the heart of Egyptian life. Thanks to a design flaw, however, his own monument is known as the "Bent Pyramid."

Solomon
Son of David and his successor as king of Israel (c.965–928 B.C.). Depicted in the Bible as a legendarily wise monarch, he built the temple at Jerusalem.

Sparta
Ancient Greek city-state in the southern Peloponnese. Sparta's formidable fighting forces became legendary; all eligible adult males were trained as soldiers.

Spring and Autumn Period
A troubled period (722–481 B.C.) of Chinese history during which the Zhou kingdom began to fragment into semiindependent states that vied with each other for power.

Step Pyramid
The earliest form of Egyptian pyramid, consisting of up to six stages, each smaller than the one below and probably representing a stairway to the heavens. The only surviving step pyramid, and probably the only one to be completed, was built for the pharaoh Djoser in around 2650 B.C. Unlike the somewhat similar ziggurats of the Sumerians, a step pyramid was built as a royal tomb rather than as a temple.

Stone Age
The period of prehistory during which people relied on stone to make tools and weaponry, the skills of metalworking being as yet undiscovered.

Stonehenge
A circular stone monument on Salisbury Plain, Wiltshire, England. Used probably as a ritual center and possibly also as an astronomical observatory, Stonehenge was built in stages over more than a thousand years, starting in around 2800 B.C. Some of the stone blocks added in the later stages weighed as much as 50 tons.

Sumerians
People of the world's earliest civilization, which was established c.3500 B.C. in the fertile land between the Tigris and Euphrates rivers in the south of present-day Iraq.

Suppululiumas I
The king who in the second half of the 14th century B.C. brought the Hittite Empire to its greatest extent, taking northern Syria from the Egyptians and dominating the Middle East.

Taharqa
A pharaoh of Nubian origin who succeeded to the Egyptian throne in c.690 B.C. After a distinguished reign Tarharqa was defeated in c.667 B.C. by an Assyrian army aided by rebellious native Egyptians.

Tangun
Mythological founder of Korea, an event traditionally dated to 2333 B.C., when Tangun is supposed to have established a kingdom at Pyongyang, the capital of present-day North Korea.

Tarquin I
An Etruscan ruler who, according to tradition, was the fifth king of Rome (c.616–578 B.C.). Tarquin I is reputed to have ordered many building works in the city, including a sewage system and the Circus Maximus, an arena for chariot racing.

Tarquin II
An Etruscan ruler who, according to tradition, was the seventh and last king of Rome (534–510 B.C.). After he was dethroned in a popular uprising, Rome was declared a republic (509 B.C.).

Thutmose I
The son of Amenhotep I and his successor as pharaoh, c.1504–1492 B.C., Thutmose I led an army into Nubia, which he subdued completely. An ensuing campaign in West Asia was less successful.

Thutmose III
Pharaoh in name from c.1479 to 25, Thutmose III in practice only came to power c.1458, his mother Hatshepsut having ruled in the early years of his reign. When he finally took over the reigns of government, he proved to be one of Egypt's great warrior pharaohs. His conquests in Nubia and West Asia brought in vast amounts of booty and helped start a fashion for art and weaponry in the Syrian style.

Tiglath-Pileser III
Ruler of Assyria from c.744 to 727 B.C. and founder of the second, or Neo-, Assyrian empire, which had its capital at Nineveh. He conquered Babylon and also subjugated Israel, Judah, and Syria.

Troy
The city famously fought over in Homer's *Iliad*. The probable site of Troy has been identified on the western coast of what is now Turkey, close to the Dardanelles Strait.

Tutankhamen
Reigning c.1333–1323 B.C., Tutankhamen came to the Egyptian throne at the age of eight. In his short reign much of the religious revolution undertaken by the heretic pharaoh Akhenaten was undone, and the worship of Egypt's old gods was restored. Today Tutankhamen is best remembered for the splendid objects found in his tomb in the Valley of the Kings, which was excavated by the British archaeologist Howard Carter in 1922.

Tyre
A Mediterranean port in modern-day southern Lebanon, Tyre was a major seaport of the Phoenician empire, famous for its silk and purple "Tyrian" dye.

Ugarit
A prosperous city-state on the coast of Syria from as early as 1500 B.C., Ugarit is remembered today mainly for the discovery of tablets on which an early form of alphabetic writing is inscribed. Ugarit may in fact have been the birthplace of the alphabet.

Upanishads
Any of some 250 Hindu sacred texts written in Sanskrit, the ancient language of India. Forming a secret doctrine, the *Upanishads* aimed to provide a mystical path to discovering truth and also introduced the idea of reincarnation.

Ur
A Sumerian city-state founded around 2900 B.C., which remained an important center under the Babylonians and Assyrians. Excavations in the early 20th century revealed a huge ziggurat and a royal cemetery containing treasures of gold, silver, and precious stones.

Urartu
First mentioned by Assyrian scribes c.1260 B.C., Urartu was a kingdom in the mountains of eastern Anatolia (modern Turkey) to the north of Assyria. In the 9th century B.C. Urartu was a real threat to the Assyrians, but its power was broken by Sargon II in c.714 B.C.

Uruk
The earliest Sumerian city, founded around 4000 B.C., Uruk has yielded some of the earliest examples of writing in the form of hundreds of inscribed clay tablets dating to about 3300 B.C.

Valley of the Kings
A secluded valley across the Nile River from the Egyptian capital of Thebes where pharaohs of the New Kingdom period chose to site their tombs. By electing to be buried in this remote spot, they hoped to avoid the attentions of tomb robbers.

Veda
Literally "books of knowledge," a series of sacred poems dating back to India's Aryan period and probably composed from c.1500 to 900 B.C. The hymns set out the ordering principles not only of Hinduism but of Aryan society in general.

Villanova Culture
An Iron Age culture named for a small town near Bologna, Italy, that flourished between 900 and 700 B.C. Skilled metalworkers, the Villanovans may have contributed to early Etruscan civilization.

Woodland Period
The time around 2000 B.C. when hunter-gatherers in the forests of eastern North America began to turn to agriculture: Modern scholars see the change as a gradual transition rather than a "Neolithic Revolution."

Wu
King of Zhou, a central Chinese province. Wu overthrew the last ruler of the Shang dynasty and founded the Zhou Dynasty, which ruled China for 800 years.

Xia Dynasty
The legendary first dynasty of China, dated c.2200–1766 B.C. Archaeological evidence suggests that the Xia rulers, if they existed, may have formed part of the Longshan Culture.

Zapotecs
Central American people who dominated an area of southern Mexico centered on the Oaxaca Valley to the west of the Mayan lands for around 1,000 years. In c.800 B.C. they developed the first hieroglyphic script yet found in the Americas.

Zhou Dynasty
The most enduring dynasty in Chinese history, which claimed to rule by the "Mandate of Heaven." In its heyday as the Western Zhou it built up political unification, but its power disintegrated during the ensuing Eastern Zhou period. It was finally overthrown in 221 B.C. by the Qin Dynasty.

ziggurat
A form of temple invented by the Sumerians and adopted by the Babylonians and other peoples of Mesopotamia. It was a stepped structure, each stage smaller than the one below, with a shrine built on the summit.

Zoroaster
Also known as Zarathustra; the founder of Zoroastrianism, who probably lived in northeastern Iran in about 600 B.C. (although some scholars place his birth much earlier, around 1200 B.C.). He revealed his divine inspiration in the *Gathas*, a set of 17 hymns that form part of the *Avesta*, the Zoroastrian holy book.

Zoroastrianism
An Iranian religion that views existence as an unending struggle between good and evil; the great creator, Ahura Mazda, is symbolized by fire. Though largely displaced by Islam, the creed survives today among the Parsi community centered in western India.

FURTHER READING

Aldred, Cyril. *Akhenaten, King of Egypt.* New York, NY: Thames & Hudson, reprint ed., 1991.

Baines, John, and Jaromir Malek. *A Cultural Atlas of Ancient Egypt.* New York, NY: Facts on File, 2000.

Bender, Barbara. *Farming in Prehistory.* London: J. Baker, 1975.

Boardman, John, Jasper Griffin, and Oswyn Murray. *The Oxford Illustrated History of Greece & the Hellenistic World.* New York, NY: Oxford University Press, 2001.

Chadwick, John. *The Mycenaean World.* New York, NY: Cambridge University Press, 1976.

Coogan, Michael David. *The Oxford History of the Biblical World.* New York, NY: Oxford University Press, 1998.

Diehl, Richard A. *The Olmecs: America's First Civilization.* New York, NY: Thames & Hudson, 2004.

Grimal, Nicolas. *A History of Ancient Egypt.* Cambridge, MA: Blackwell, reprint ed., 1994.

Haynes, Sybille. *Etruscan Civilization: A Cultural History.* Los Angeles, CA: J. Paul Getty Museum, 2000.

Hopper, R.J. *The Early Greeks.* New York, NY: Barnes and Noble, 1976.

Johanson, Donald, and Blake Edgar. *From Lucy to Language.* New York, NY: Simon & Schuster Editions, 1996.

Jones, Steve. ed. *The Cambridge Encyclopedia of Human Evolution.* New York, NY: Cambridge University Press, reprint ed., 1994.

Kemp, Barry J. *Ancient Egypt: Anatomy of a Civilization.* New York, NY: Routledge, reprint ed., 2005.

Kramer, Samuel N. *The Sumerians: Their History, Culture, and Character.* Chicago, IL: University of Chicago Press, 1971.

Leakey, Richard. *The Origin of Humankind.* HarperCollins Publishers, reprint ed., 1996.

McIntosh, Jane. *A Peaceful Realm: The Rise and Fall of the Indus Civilization.* Boulder, CO: Westview Press, 2001.

Matthews, Victor. *A Brief History of Ancient Israel.* Louisville, KY: Westminster John Knox Press, 2002.

Oppenheim, A. Leo. *Ancient Mesopotamia: Portrait of a Dead Civilization.* Chicago, IL: University of Chicago Press, 1977.

Possehl, Gregory L. *The Indus Civilization: A Contemporary Perspective.* Walnut Creek, CA: Altamira Press, 2003.

Reeves, Nicholas. *The Complete Tutankhamun: The King, The Tomb, The Royal Treasure.* New York, NY: Thames & Hudson, 1990.

Roux, Georges. *Ancient Iraq.* New York, NY: Penguin Books, 3rd ed., 1992.

Saggs, H.W.F. *The Greatness That Was Babylon: A Survey of the Ancient Civilization of the Tigris–Euphrates Valley.* London: Sidgwick and Jackson, 1988.

Shanks, Hershel, ed. *Ancient Israel.* Washington, DC: Biblical Archaeology Society, 1999.

Stringer, Chris, and Robin McKie. *African Exodus: The Origins of Modern Humanity.* New York, NY: Henry Holt, 1997.

Thapar, Romila. *Early India: From the Origins to A.D. 1300.* Berkeley, CA: University of California Press, 2003.

Torelli, Mario, ed. *Etruscans.* New York, NY: Rizzoli, 2001.

Waley, Arthur. *Three Ways of Thought in Ancient China.* Stanford, CA: Stanford University Press, reprint ed., 1983.

SET INDEX